PHOTOGRAPH BY: LEO DICKINSON

# A CRAG RATS TALE

BY

ALAN 'RICHARD' MCHARDY

•••

Published by Monkey Gone To Heaven

First Published 2011

.....

Set in 10/12/20 pt Bembo

Designed and Typeset by Monkey Gone To Heaven
www.monkeygonetoheaven.co.uk
Printed in Scotland by J.Thomson Colour Printers

...

PAPERBACK
ISBN: 978-0-9570563-0-5

Monkey Gone To Heaven is committed
to a sustainable future.
The book in your hands is made from 50% recycled paper certified
by the
Forest Stewardship Council.

••

V

# PART ONE

...

# PART TWO

•••

# FORWARD

•••

This book is an honest, humorous and amazing account of this remarkable man's life.

It takes you on a thrilling roller coaster ride that is the chosen lifestyle of Richard and his wife Barbara.

Richard started his working life as an apprentice joiner in North Manchester in the early 1950s. In a tough environment there was little or no spare money for sporting activities that weren't considered the norm.

Fortunately, he discovered the hills and crags of the Peak District which gave him the freedom he needed in his teenage years. He quickly learned the basic skills of rock climbing and later made regular trips to North Wales and The Lakes and spent his summer holidays in the Alps with like minded friends he had met − all remarkable characters described as the pages unfold.

In 1964, a crashing fall whilst climbing in North Wales would seem to put an end to his dream. What follows is a truly amazing story of the grit and determination of this larger than life character.

I got to know Richard in 1967 and the following years gave me the very best of times climbing with Richard on the crags of Britain and in the Alps, doing the hardest routes of the time in fine style.

Without doubt, Richard is one of Britain's most respected and leading climbers of his generation. He has told his story as many hoped he would. The reader could be sat with him, listening to his endless storytelling with a brew or a pint of beer.

This is a captivating account of his life as a climber/mountaineer shared with Barbara and their two sons Alan and Ian.


Paul Braithwaite 'Tut'

To
Barbara McHardy
With Love

# I

## HOME OPENSHAW MANCHESTER 1950s

The consultant spoke with the clarity and tone of a judge. 'No climbing ladders, no driving cars and definitely no climbing mountains, the result of the test confirm that both your periods of unconsciousness were due to an epileptic seizure.' He did not seem to think that my work as a joiner involved much risk so I never bothered to sign on the sick, I did give up climbing for six months. At twenty five my life had irrevocably changed, not big time like losing a leg or going blind but still irrevocably changed. For some ludicrous reason I felt ashamed. All I knew of Epilepsy was how it was perceived by the ordinary person in the street. The practicalities of coping; whether to tell an employer or to carry on rock climbing were minor compared with feeling that I had become mentally defective. Such was the effect on me of prejudiced opinion at the time. But let me go back in time twelve or thirteen years.

My Parents house, like many houses sixty years ago had a tin bath which we used in front of the fire. When I was about twelve the roof got repaired, prior to which it leaked badly mostly into my bedroom. The toilet was outside and in winter a paraffin lamp kept it from freezing, combined with the white wash that covered its walls the place had a nice smell. Sitting on the bog was atmospheric and with the scraps of newspaper that stood in place of bog role the place even had stuff to read. On cold nights in particular sound travels and some of the factories and the railways worked through the night. Eva brothers and Masseys were both drop forge works and they were the noisiest. A shrieking noise followed by a massive thump as metal was pummelled into shape. Daytimes in midweek, the streets would be almost deserted; most people were working in factories on a 48-hour week plus overtime. In between a factory and the front of our houses there was a tip and an unfenced reservoir. The factory which owned the reservoir had dumped all sorts of waste around it, some of it was fairly toxic. Even after a little girl drowned they refused to erect a fence. To one side of the houses was a canal with a chemical works on the other side. There were old barges laid up from before the war with lots of rats scuttling around them. There were often dead dogs that had been stuffed in a bag and flung in the water to save the cost of being put to sleep with a vet. Lots of kids got into minor trouble with the law before they had left school and some progressed to being criminals. My grandfather had a small holding about four miles away where he bred pigs. Until he died when I was eleven years old I spent every available minute there. Eventually we got a new landlord who had our roof repaired. With the house dry my Mother bought some new carpet and wallpaper, my Dad made a bugger of the wallpapering, no one-piece lining up with another but the streaks of dirty brown glue gave it an artistic touch. The carpet was a bigger disaster, when he had finished it was in seventeen separate pieces, my Mum cried. One time he nicked a five gallon tin of dark green engine paint from work and painted all the doors, the toilet seat and a bath we had just installed in the scullery. With no preparation the paint took ages to dry, he finished up with a green ring on his arse the rest of us touched the seat first. The paint job he did on the bath ran down the sides and pooled in the bottom. He usually worked a seven-day twelve-hour shift as a labourer in a foundry and lacked time or energy for domestic work. He could however recite huge long Robert Service monologues about the Yukon in the gold rush days of the 19th century—they must have transported his soul into a more interesting world. When I was thirteen a friend got me to join the air cadets with him. Although I was scarcely more than five foot tall they put me on guard duty with an old Lee Enfield rifle with no bullets, some kids came taking the mickey, they were bigger than me so full of bluff I took aim, one of them collapsed in tears the others ran off. This made me feel quite hard. A week later the guy who instructed Judo grabbed hold of me behind a shed and planted his sloppy lips over my face, feeling less like a gunman and more like a pretty boy, I left the cadets. Previous to this they arranged with an experienced walker to take a group of us hiking in Derbyshire. The rucksack I had was ex-army and designed for carrying ammunition, it was heavy even when it was empty. My Mother thought I was off to Antarctica and filled a huge tin full of cheese butties, it then weighed a ton. I was only five foot two the sack was three foot and about half my weight. From Glossop we caught a bus to Hayfield got off in the middle of nowhere and climbed over a fence. At first there was no path, only a wilderness of deep heather, with me being bent double carrying the massive sack I could hardly see over it. By the side of Kinder Reservoir those of us with short legs were relieved to find a good path which went up by William Clough then over a watershed and onto the peaty head waters of the Ashop River. For us coming from the inner city this was an entirely alien world, eerily silent but for the sound of trickling water in the gullies and the croaking noise of the grouse. City people are often agoraphobic, certainly my Dad was and so were most of our group as they walked in a dumb silence. On the other side of the river the ground went steeply uphill to meet a dark rock face which ran along the horizon for a couple of miles. This was the north edge of the Kinder Scout plateau which is formed by a triangle of steep sides enclosing a wilderness of peat and heather. Years before when the landowners were trying to deny access to hill walkers they encouraged the idea that some of the bogs on the plateau were deep enough for people to disappear into. Our leader having told us about this, forgot to tell us it was an exaggeration, so scared witless we walked silently on until we came across the Snake Pass road and within a few hundred yards the Snake Inn. The Pub had at the time a cafe for hill walkers, a brew went down well but too knackered to eat I gave most of my dry cheese butties away, more to lighten the load than in any spirit of generosity. Going west the road climbs and then crosses Feather Bed Moss and then on down to Glossop. Not far from the high point of the road we took to the moor and after a few hundred yards a roman road, perfectly exposed from the surrounding peat appeared, there are grooves in the stones which hundreds of chariots must have carved. After a long descent we arrived in Glossop, tired, happy and amazed that such wild places were virtually on our doorsteps. I repeated this walk five times before leaving school. On one occasion I changed my route and went onto Kinder Scouts western edge, it was a lovely hot and sunny day. By Kinder Downfall I saw three people rock climbing, two men and one woman. All the women I knew spent their spare time drinking tea and eating fudge. I had a pathological fear of heights but wedged behind some boulders fifty feet from the edge I watched the silent proceedings. I thought cricket was dangerous but dangling on a thin hemp rope above a big drop seemed completely nutty. Walking the moors of the Dark Peak had now become a burning ambition, so different from the big city. Finding people to go walking with was difficult, several school friends tried but the silence, emptiness and effort did not appeal to them. Also in our social class there was pressure to conform and never rock the boat by doing, or even reading anything unusual. Walkers and climbers were usually individualistic, they had to be to ignore convention and do their own thing. Most young men of the time became Teddy Boys. Rock and Roll had started before Elvis Presley by groups such as Bill Haley with numbers like *Rock Around the clock*. The clothes were weird; long jackets and drain pipe trousers. The haircuts had a large Quiff at the front and a DA or 'ducks arse' at the back. The dancing was energetic and the evening always finished with a fight or a snog in a dirty back alley. Not very keen on scrapping for a sport or having sex among the dog shit, that first day out walking with the cadets had shown me something else.

# 2

## EDALE 1956

Leaving school was sad, hardly educated and with an uncertain future all thirty of us had gone through ten years together not doing a tap and were now expected to conjure up a work ethic from nowhere. We attended a compulsory church service in Manchester Cathedral and said our sad goodbyes in a coffee bar. Work was different than I had anticipated. Seven thirty starts and half five finishes did come hard at first but the work was interesting and the company of grown men better than School. The practical part of being an apprentice fitter I found easy but day release at the technical college was impossibly difficult. At school we had known almost every Hymn in the Church hymn book but little else. The maths that was part of an HNC course on the other hand was totally over my head. After ten months I left Crossleys and became an apprentice joiner along with a more practically based City & Guilds course. Changing trades was a step in the dark as I had enjoyed the work at Crossleys. When they had a massive diesel engine on test the noise made the whole works vibrate. It felt important. These engines were designed to go in a trailer and provide emergency electricity in the event of a nuclear war. Waiting at the stores one day I got talking to another apprentice, he said he went walking and had got to know a gang of other teenagers who went out to Edale every weekend. The following Saturday I went with him. The path from Hayfield is scenic enough until we arrived on a col and looked down on a narrow green dale enclosed on both sides by big steep hillsides. It was a life changing moment. There were two older guys among the group, Stan Potter and another guy, Bill who had not long returned from Egypt after the abortive war over the Suez Canal. They had an arrangement with a farmer to use an old barn as a club hut. Stan had club cards made, little blue things with Medlock Climbing Club in black. Coopers cafe was the social base in Edale; half of the building was an old railway carriage without wheels. On a weekend the cafe would get full of walkers straight down from Kinder Scout, the smell of wet clothing and cigarettes vying with the smell of chicory essence which was, back then, used as a substitute for coffee. We spent more time doing the barn up than walking. Then one Saturday Potter dragged us all up a climb on a cliff called Upper Tor. When Potter disappeared the gang fell apart but not before one of the lads, Tony Hunt, had got the climbing bug. He talked me into going with him, I did but I was not much use. We would hang about at the bottom of Laddow Rocks, Yellow Slacks or Upper Tor and eventually some climbers would take Tony up a climb. I was scared just sitting looking down the hill under the crag. Sometimes some motherly type women, not taking no for an answer, would drag me up something really easy. Tony bought a hemp rope. The usual drivel about mother's washing line is bullshit. If you had a washing line longer than eight foot then you had a garden with parents rich enough to tap up for some dosh to buy a hemp rope. We had no slings or karabiners but we still managed to climb some easy routes. One Sunday afternoon in late September 1956, we met up with three of the old team, Keith Taylor, Pete Bamfield and Dave Upton. Pete Bamfield suggested we made a new club. He even had a name for it, the Alpha club. He had the idea for the name from a climb he had read about in Wales 'Alpha slab'. A week or two later Alan Parker and Ralph Harris 'Rastus', turned the five of us into seven. A month or two later Keith sat smoking his pipe under Castle Naze when a lad fell off a climb knocking the pipe out of Keith's mouth — Brian Barlow and his mate Pete

Baldwin joined the club. They were apprentice tool makers at Reynolds Chains, but a friend of theirs Les Brown had gone to University. Les was on the first ascent of Nuptse, a peak over 25,000 ft just west of Everest and went on to put up many new rock routes. He was a member of the Manchester University Mountaineering Club and he became our contact with the greater climbing fraternity. Within a few years the Alpha club went on to contribute hundreds of first ascents and, in the case of Craig Gogarth, a completely new crag. In the early days I was the youngest and smallest and was often doing thick tricks as a consequence my name was changed from Alan McHardy to Dick McThick. When I became less of a callow youth the Dick became Richard. One winter Sunday I got stuck scrambling up the easy descent route into the Amphitheatre section of the crag at Kinder Downfall. This was where I had first seen rock climbers in action two years before. Pete Bamfield told me that the only reason I came out was for company and I would never make a climber. Walking back to Edale over the Kinder plateau I slipped and fell into the icy Kinder river, I was wet, feeling humiliated and depressed, but I decided that on balance the very beauty of the place made everything worthwhile. On our way down Grindsbrooke, Brian Barlow insisted I follow him up a slab on Grindsbrooke Rocks without a rope and with Tony Hunt climbing last we got up and my mood was transformed. On the train home I fantasized about the future. Three years later I took Pete up Diagonal Route on Dinas Mot, a Hard Very Severe in Llanberis Pass. By then I was happy at the grade and had a wry smile. Pete had played an important part in my transformation into a climber, just as Brian had.

Our love affair with Edale and Kinder Scout had a lot to do with our having the barn as a doss and also the piano in the Church Hotel. Keith had a popular selection of music that he could play which gave us plenty of brownie points with the locals; some of us were too young to be drinking so we needed them. The climbing on Kinder was very often cold and wet also the rock is rounded and badly protected. Protection in those days was comprised of chock stones, rock spikes or trees which on Kinder were in short supply. This led us to spread our wings and try other places such as the Roaches. From a climbers perspective the peak district is formed of Millstone Grit, Kinder Grit, Limestone and the unusual kind of sandy grit that the Roaches are made of. From the top of the Roaches it is easy to see the hill farm that my great grandfather was evicted from in the 1890s and which my grandfather tried all his life to earn enough money to buy back, but failed. The nearest pub was called the New Inn and had not changed since the days when my great grandfather had frequented the place. The beer was brought up from the cellar in big enamel jugs, paraffin lamps and candles were the only lighting. Several years later the place was gutted and given a new name. It became posh and we were not welcome. The first time I saw the Roaches the sky was clear blue, the rock was red in places and underneath were bright green trees. Over time these trees became scabby and the wild wallabies that inhabited the place were hunted to extinction; they had escaped from a zoo years before. One Sunday I seconded Keith up three of the classic easy routes and was really chuffed. The lot of us missed the bus and had to walk all the way to Buxton over Axe edge. After dark a full moon came out, pounding the tarmac for miles with only thin pumps on my feet became painful but I felt that I could make a climber. It had been a magic day. It was Stanage Edge that really took our fancy, hundreds of climbs of all grades on friendlier rock than Kinder or the Roaches. The nearest railway station to Stanage is in Hathersage where there was a cafe run by an old lady, originally from south Wales. She was ace. Years before we had met her she had had all her teeth pulled out at once with the result that she resembled a hen with her nose and chin nearly touching. To assert authority she would shout 'Feet off chairs,' in a high pitched voice. Seventeen years later she showed me a photo of her wedding, she had been beautiful. We started sleeping in a cave on Stanage and eating Ma Thomas's cheap but horrendous food. We talked her into buying a chip making machine but she never had the fat hot enough and the chips came out white and full of grease. Some of the lads got a fixation with doing first ascents. One enterprise was on Dovestones quarry. Pete Bamfield was belaying Keith as he battled his way up steep loose rock. He had to use several pitons for aid and in the process dislodged a lot of rock. They shouted to me to move position on the lower belay ledge, Keith was about to dislodge a big rock. It destroyed the ledge where I had been sitting. We all got up the route and they called it Jericho Wall. I soled the climb again in the late sixties, it was then a good sound route but unfortunately the Quarry is now too loose to climb on.

A repetitive job at work made my right elbow painful and impossible to straighten. The lads had an answer to this and threw a rope over a beam in the barn and had me hang from the rafters until I fell off. This was supposed to make me less afraid of falling off and might fix my elbow. They had had some success with Al after he complained about a bad back, rubbing rancid butter on him cured the problem. The real reason for the trouble with my elbow had a long Latin name but after the operation my elbow lost 60% of its movement and a tiny bit of my forearms rotation. This reduced the reach in my right arm and made lay backing in a left facing corner awkward; my elbow pushes my hand out of reach of a crack. I also could never train my upper arm to be as strong as it would have been if it had its full range of movement. Three years later I started going to a weight lifting club with Bob Brigham of climbing shop fame. Bob was into cycling and skiing and wanted to work on his leg strength, and I thought the weights would strengthen my elbow. The place was a mutton head's paradise. I adored it. Running up the dark stairs one night my vision was entirely filled by massive jet black bicep. Earl Maynard was a Mr Universe but had stood back on the landing to let me pass, a gentle giant. Another guy was the top Orthopaedic Surgeon at Salford Royal Infirmary. McQueen was unusual for a surgeon, being just like the rest of us—a red neck. His ambitions included being Mr Britain over forty and climbing the Matterhorn although he was not a climber. I badly strained my good left elbow climbing on Curber edge so McQueen fixed me an appointment at the Hospital. I took a seat at the end of a large queue, and it was clear that many of the others had some serious defects. Between us and the doctor was just a green sheet, I felt a wimp coming back from X-ray with pictures of a mildly arthritic elbow but my name was called next and I walked from the back to the front of the queue. Once behind the green sheet McQueen said in a loud voice that he had bench pressed three hundred pound the night before. The people waiting could hear everything.

For all his eccentricity he was probably ahead of the game in knowing the value of training muscles to protect joints. Fifteen years later I damaged my left elbow working as casual labourer unloading a ship; then neither of my elbows would straighten. Gritstone is a good but difficult rock to climb on, and even so-called easy routes are often hard and dangerous, so technically by the June of 1957 even I was getting more competent. However Grits relatively small scale meant that we were not learning to deal with very exposed places and the nervous energy involved in multi-pitch routes. We had a very good Easter in the Ogwen valley in North Wales then ambition got the better of Bamfield and we all went to the Isle of Skye for our summer holidays. Out of the frying pan and into the fire.

SGURR MHIC CHOINNICH, SGURR THEARLAICH, SGURR ALASDAIR

# 3

## SKYE 1957

The most comprehensive view of the Cuillin Mountains is from near Elgol, which is situated to the south east. They form a continuous bow shaped line of peaks and from that side, the whole of the ridge is mostly visible. They are unlike any other hills in Britain. Above the initial slopes there is no grass, the ground is either, steep scree glaciated boiler plates or big rock faces, topped off by a precipitous ridge that runs from Sgurr nan Gillean in the north to Gars-Bheinn at the south end of the ridge. This last peak plunges 3000 ft into the sea in one massive rocky slope. In between these two peaks the ridge links eleven Munros. We had travelled overnight from Manchester, the train arriving in Mallaig about mid-day. Mallaig was a busy fishing port and it was from here that the ferry departed to cross the Sound of Sleat to Armadale on the very south of Skye. After crossing on the ferry we would have had to travel from Armadale to Glen Brittle by various buses which would have taken all day. The weather was glorious, fairly windy, warm and sunny. Some other lads had been negotiating with a local fisherman and he had offered to take all of us from Mallaig on the mainland to Glen Brittle on Skye for 12 / 6d each, including a few brews. Once over the sound of Sleat the fishing boat with its bow cutting through the waves was passing in between the small island of Soay and a mass of steep brown gabbro plunging deep into the sea. Since Easter my climbing standard had improved but on closer proximity to the Cuillins I knew I was going to be out of my depth. I was sinking into a gloomy state when I heard the captain shouting 'Whale to Starboard!' She was no Moby Dick running for her life. Instead she sat calmly with her body half out of the sea, not a care in the world, her body reflecting the brown of the rock behind her. The contrast between this and Manchester was stark. There was no pier at Glen Brittle, the sand was blackish coloured and the water knee deep where we landed. The youth hostel was a mile or two away, standing in a bleak setting the only trees in sight were around Glen Brittle House half a mile back. The plantations that are now there have been planted and in some cases felled and grown again in the years since. Willy Sutherland and his elder brother were the wardens. Willy was thick set and gruff, his brother was thin with a caustic sense of humour. The main scene of our operations was in Coire Lagan, the path from the Hostel ascended up by a stream as if going to Coire na Banachdich, passed a large waterfall and traversed south east past a small Loch often knee deep in wet peat. The stone covered Coire Lagan is a marvellous site. Boiler plate slabs guard the upper coire where nestles a small green lochain surrounded by huge loose cliffs. After doing a climb on Sgurr Sgumain and a brush with a very scary ridge immediately afterwards, Pete Bamfield, Al myself and Rastus decided to do a route on Sgurr Alasdair, the biggest of the Cuillin peaks the next day.

Collie's Climb 270 m grade diff. Much of the climb is basalt, and, in the main, loose. Near the top somebody had scrawled on the rock in large letters 'Doctor Collie is a Cunt.' — Not really fair, as Collie had done the first ascent in 1906 when there were few other climbs and it must have been a very worthwhile achievement, but none the less the climb is a heap of shit. Scared but pleased we arrived on the summit. My relief was short lived as Bamfield and Al Parker announced that we were all going to traverse over Sgurr Thearlaich, Sgurr Mhic Choinnich and onto Sgurr Dearg with the intention of climbing the Inaccessible

Pinnacle. Although the thought filled me with dread the reality was even worse. The ridge between us and the In Pin was very exposed. Pete gave me a kick up my arse whenever I crawled on my hands and knees. Strangely once at the In Pin things went fine and I even led through. Abseiling down the short side was my second abseil. At the bottom I was immensely pleased but a nervous wreck. Then Pete announced another objective and off they went. Not for me, I made my way off the ridge down Coire Banachdich and slowly and happily back to the Youth Hostel. By the time we had been at the hostel two days I had broken my plate and lost my knife and fork but I still had a plastic cup and a spoon. Starving hungry and with hours to wait for the rest of the lads to appear, I took a tin of soup from our supplies and using my plastic cup instead of a pan put the soup to warm up on the hostel's Rayburn like stove. 'Is that your cup on the stove?' The speaker was a bonny girl about my own age. This was a pleasant surprise, and maybe even a chat up line, but her next words were 'You should go and see it.' Why could it not have been some fatherly old man with the news? On the hot plate was a blue blob with burnt soup around the edge. The thin sarcastic warden took the piss but now I was without a cup.

The sky was blue and we were going to catch a boat around to the other side of the ridge, where Loch Coruisk empties into the sea. The wardens knew we were in a hurry so they left us until last to give us our cleaning jobs and then announced the weather would be bad by the afternoon. Our objective was the Dubh Ridge of Sgurr Dubh Beag, described thus in the present guide book:

*'This is the best easy climb in Skye and a contender for the best easy climb in Britain, 920 m moderate.'*

From the top of the climb our planned route went over Sgurr Dubh Mor across the dreaded Dubh Gap and down the Alasdair stone shoot into Coire Lagan and back to Glen Brittle. The previous winter we would crawl into our sleeping bags in some manky doss close to where we were climbing. Bamfield would read out loud a chapter from Herman Buhl's classic epic *Nanga Parbat Pilgrimage*. Our proposed day would be a doddle, a warm up for greater things if we were ever to follow our hero's footsteps. That at least that was the kind of fantasies that entered my mind. After about half a mile walk along a path at the side of Loch Coruisk I stepped into a bog. It is rare to go above your knees in British Bogs but I went up to my waist in this one. The others found this hilarious but within a couple of hours the forecast of rain was correct and then we were all soaking wet. Before the weather turned nasty came the Dubh slabs—hundreds of feet of easy angled rough gabbro, so easy that we did not need a rope. For a while the sun continued to shine, highlighting the light brown sweep of rock with the dark waters of Loch Coruisk and the green sea beyond. Our scramble finished on a kind of pinnacle and after a short abseil continued up steeper rock. By the time we found the Dubh Gap the visibility was very poor and the rain hard. Abseiling into the gap my anorak became caught in between the rope and karabiner which everybody used in conjunction with a sit sling for abseiling. I was stuck, and I was the last one down. After bouncing about it came free and with a torn anorak I joined the lads in the Gap. The climb out the other side was by now a waterfall. Only Al was good enough to climb it. Not normally given to brave or masochistic feats, he fought his way to the top. Pete, me and Rastus all needed a tight rope to follow him. Bamfield found the top of the Alasdair stone shoot and we were soon in Coire Lagan happy beyond words, singing the song '*for we are jolly good fellows*' in praise of Al's act of bravery and Pete's navigation.

Before we left for home myself and Rastus climbed Cioch west. This is a classic of a climb which would have been well beyond us at the start of our holiday. It was wet and on the third pitch I got off route and after a hundred foot traversed a thin slab with no protection. Not sure I could get back on to the route I pressed on and found more bottle than I thought I possessed. This was a revelation to me and one that meant so much. Thus far I had been the whipping boy: often scared silly and doing thick tricks. After our Skye trip everything seemed possible. Me and Rastus hitch-hiked home and on route stayed in Glencoe youth hostel. A large German man saw our rope and in heavily accented English asked us if we knew of the great Herman Buhl. Yes he is our hero, we told him. 'He is dead' he said and started to cry.

Some years later Rastus was for some reason sectioned and spent the rest of his life in a mental institute before killing himself. He was a good friend with not a nasty bone in his body and with a gift to see the humour in anything. I hope that he got as much pleasure from our Skye trip as I did. There was something special starting out climbing like we all did, rather than going on a course or being guided. Every new place had to be explored, every new improvement in our climbing standard felt like our own personal Everest.

ALPHA GROUP, 1959

# 4

'58 and '59

Stanage edge had become our new venue, three miles of
solid Millstone Grit. Al Parker was never one for too much
discomfort, and after a few good forays into alpinism decided to
forgo the bigger mountains and concentrated on Grit. Starting
in 1958 he has done in the region of 197 new climbs, most
of them on Stanage.

Robin Hoods cave is half way up the crag and so was never
covered in sheep shit—making it a perfect doss, but it was a long
way from the Pub. It did get other visitors though: Norman
the Arab would tell us about the fourth dimension and John
Henry Phearon would make guest appearances having come
down from Bradford. John was an electrician in a coal mine,
his accent was almost impossible to understand and he swore
all the time. One Saturday evening he appeared with a blonde
lady, ever so nice, she seemed too nice to be sleeping in a cave.
He helped her up into the cave, brewed drinkable tea and
generally behaved like a gentleman. Ten years later I met John
in the Fox house pub, he and Olga were married and he had
become a University Lecturer. They seemed happy together
and did not give me the impression of fanatical class warriors
so it left me intrigued when John said, referring to his years
working down the Pit, 'If we knew then what I know now
there'd have been a revolution.'

Some of the original club gave up climbing and others appeared.

For me a period of consolidation followed our Skye trip. Gritstone is the perfect place to learn crack climbing techniques and having to keep a cool head when all you have for holds are rounded creases and a grinning floor. Stan and Alan Goodwin, Jim Smith, Andy Garvey and then Bob Brayshaw appeared. Bob was ahead of his time. A reach close on ten feet, very strong fingers and excellent technique made his potential huge. Two of his new routes on Stanage stand out, one is called Daydreamer E2 6b and the other is Desperation E1 5c, both nearly impossible for a short person, both done in 1959. Brian Barlow and Brian Platt had bought motorbikes which soon became our mode of transport. By the autumn of 58 a fifteen year old called Paul Nunn appeared. Initially I met him on the Roaches and the following week he cycled from his home in Macclesfield over the cat and fiddle road through Buxton and on to Hathersage. He soon put away his catholic principles and fiddled the train like the rest of us. In time his granny bought him a motorbike. He was not very safe. Fifty years later Barlow remarked that Paul's granny would have been safer buying him a shotgun.

We started cooking at the crag instead of going down to Hathersage and being slowly poisoned in Ma Thomas's cafe. We all brought different ingredients making spaghetti one week and egg and chips the next. On a summer evening it meant that we often had the best of the day sat about in the heather watching the sunset. A book that had influence on me at the time was High Heaven by Jacques Boell. Our first hero Herman Buhl had a great desire for masochistic neck stretching, but for the Frenchman Boell the mountains were entirely spiritual. One of the best Scots climbers of his day was Pat Walsh, a member of the rough tough Creagh Dhu climbing club from Glasgow. One day on Stanage he told me his personal attitude to the hills—and oddly they were more akin to Boell than to the Austrian Buhl. Pat made the point that with the current lack of protection, people had to work through the grades before tackling the hardest climbs. He thought this ensured that only people who really loved the hills would stay the course. His thinking was that if protection improved, climbing would become a mass sport, primarily competitive. This has been most obviously true.

Brayshaw was excessively competitive and would be insufferable when he got one over on us. This led the rest of us to do some crazy stunts in our attempts to keep up with him. Al Parker did some very thin moves to climb Count's Buttress Direct without any runners, a fall from which would have been serious. Bob was the only one of us to have successfully top roped the climb; a practice we seldom did. He sensibly backed off leading it whereas Al made a suicidal leap from a small foothold to gain a rounded horizontal crack with the tips of his fingers. On another occasion both Bob and Al had led the Right Unconquerable. The next morning Paul went to Mass in Hathersage and me and Al stayed in our sleeping bags. Bob went off into the rain. After Paul got back we had a brew then left the cave and went to look at the Unconquerable's. Bob was already there, sat with his back against a rock looking incredibly smug. There was a good chock stone about half way up, I decided to do without, tied onto the rope threw my runners on the floor and set off lay backing. Having no PA rock shoes we either climbed in boots or black rubber pumps. Half way up my pumps began to slip away from me on the green wet wall and in extremis I searched my mind for an idea on how to stay on. The answer was in my memory; a picture in the guide book of Joe Brown doing the first ascent in 1949. With his old army jacket on he was hanging on the flake exactly where I was, but he had his left foot pointing in at the crack. Copying this picture gave my feet more traction and stopped me slipping off. However, it proved nothing; Bob was still a better climber.

The next two years seemed to hang in a pleasant bubble, a time

AUTHOR LEADING 'SURPRISE' BELAYED BY BRIAN PLATT, BOB BRAYSHAW WATCHING. STANAGE 1959

PHOTOGRAPH BY: ANDY GARVEY

capsule with very little to worry about other than becoming a better climber. Work was just about looking forward to the next brew time and enjoying learning from the men, most of whom had been through the war. Buying my own transport or getting in a relationship with a girl was not something my mind or finances could cope with. Life was blissfully simple. Our sleeping bags ended at chest level and bits of cut down blanket did the rest. When Paul Nunn appeared he already had a Blacks Icelandic sleeping bag. My conversion to saving and spending came after watching him consistently have a good night's sleep. After this I went one better than Paul and bought an Icelandic Special. Al went one better and bought a Polar. Paul then got some PA rock boots. These boots were made in Paris and were truly amazing. They deservedly had a monopoly of the market for years. Paul's were two sizes too big for me but he charged 2 shillings and 6 pence a go, one route only. The cost was equal to egg, chips and beans in Ma Thomas's. The only importer of these shoes at the time was Arvon's climbing shop in Bethesda. The Easter of 1959 five of us deviated from our journey to Llanberis Pass and got some of our own. I can honestly say that without PAs I would not have climbed for that much longer. Boots and pumps had no finesse. In boots you could not feel small footholds very well. Pumps were useless on small sharp holds. PAs truly transformed climbing. After our visit to Arvon's shop me and John Smith got to the Pass and climbed Phantom Rib and Spectre, our first VS leads away from Gritstone. My next buy was a Blacks Arctic Guinea tent bought direct from Blacks factory in Greenock—shop soiled it was cheap but in Glasgow slang, magic. Our Jean's Christmas present that year was on our front room floor when I got home from Derbyshire, one Sunday night before Christmas. It was a blown up lilo but my Mum could not comprehend what it was for, 'How do you get in it' she had sat for hours looking at it without realizing it was used for sleeping on not in. Barlow nearly got killed falling off his BSA Road Rocket so he bought a Vincent 1000 from Hugh Banner. For road handling it was not as good as the Road Rocket but the big Vincent could, on the way back from the pub, fit three of us on it. Platty and Al bought Velocet Venoms they were only 500cc but had very good road holding. Paul Nunn, a year later, bought a 250cc BSA which he swapped for a Gold Flash, his Granny was certainly generous. At work I had a six month period, late '58 early '59 working in Manchester Town Hall and the nearby Central Library with an old joiner, Alf Winterbottom. Alf had been a climber before the War and had known famous climbers on the scene such as Alf Bridge. I could never really get Alf to tell me any stories, maybe the memories of those pre-war days climbing and gallivanting around the hills were too precious to let slip, but he took a quiet pleasure in my activities. That would have seemed only conjecture except for one occasion. On the Christmas Eve, Paul and I were catching the evening bus to Keswick. Paul was coming straight from School and meeting me at the Library. Alf had got his wife to make a pile of mince pies and after a small feast he wished us on our way. That night we walked from Keswick down Borrowdale and camped in the rain on Stye Head pass. The next day we climbed Napes Needle and Needle Ridge in the rain and years later his description of that day is included in Ken Wilson's excellent book *Classic Rock*. That evening in the Wasdale Head barn we had powdered potatoes and corned beef for our Christmas dinner whilst a club from London filled the barn with borrowed tables and chairs and scoffed their way through a feast. Next day Rastus turned up with the club funds, which gave us a Boxing Day high tea at a nearby farm and two pints each in the pub.

Except for one week of rain, the summer of 1959 was fantastic. By the autumn the back of my climbing shirt was threadbare with the sun. At the Easter we had all started to lead VS, on volcanic rock, the years on grit were now paying off. For my summer holidays Paul and I went to Scotland arriving on a late Sunday afternoon to a warm completely dry Glencoe. Two Creagh Dhu guys offered us the use of their club hut, Jacksonville, which is right under the Buachaille Etive Mor. As they left for Glasgow they had recommended Raven's Gully, this must have been because for once that century it was dry. In the night it began to rain and after four days of torrential downpour we could only cross the river with great difficulty. When the sun eventually appeared we went to try our luck with the Gully. This was a bit thick and after we had both got washed off the crux we went off to Ben Nevis. One trip up the Allt a' Mhuilinn with the camping and climbing gear was not enough so we returned to Fort William and struggled back up the path with two rucksacks full of tinned food, we planned to stay a while. For our first climb we intended climbing Tower ridge by doing a climb on the massive Douglas Boulder to start. We were sat on the top of the Boulder when after only two days respite the rain returned. Unable to carry the camping gear, climbing stuff and grub we sat and ate our way through one week's food. We then went south to meet up with the rest of the lads in Wales, Paul on his motorbike; he was still a learner and me on the train. By the time I got to Wales Paul was climbing with Bob. The summer holiday was a disappointment, but I did make a dam in the stream with a seventeen-year old Martin Boysen.

In September Roy Fryer and I went to Langdale. The description in the 1950 Langdale guide book of Kipling Groove was a masterpiece of scary description, so much so that after reading it in the pub we did not read it again. Hence the following epic. '*The next move is the crux. A strenuous arm-pull brings a diagonal crack above the overhang within reach, followed by a horizontal crack a little higher to the right. The latter is used first to surmount the overhang and then as a mantelshelf, foot holds being almost non-existent. Traverse right to a resting place at the foot of a thin crack.*' Having achieved this contortion instead of stepping right

A LANGDALE LADS WEDDING

I went left, above was a mossy wall capped by an overhang with no sign of it having ever been climbed. I still had not bothered to learn how to tie a bowline, instead I used a sling and small screw gate karabiner around my waist with an overhand knot clipped into the karabiner, making in the event of a fall a three way pull on the karabiner. Les Brown had mentioned to me the likely drawbacks to this and now with the last runner a long way below and being off route his words came back to haunt me. I was now stuck and unable to reverse when a young Mick Burke appeared in the Gully below, he assured me I was on route and then sat down to watch. He knew very well I was not. The moss was dry and acted like small ball bearings for both hands and feet. Over to the right looked impossible, I was above the point of being able to see where I should have been. At the top of the wall was a bulge, I teetered up the wall on sloping holds not knowing what to expect. A V-shaped little groove cut the overhang to the left of where I arrived. With no way to step across to it I was left with no alternative but to do a totally blind lunge hoping to find a hold over the overhang good enough to allow a pull and a swing left into the groove.

My hand sank into a jug. A fall from these moves would have been in excess of eighty feet onto a ten year old piton. Years later with sit harnesses, belay plates and better protection going off route would not have been as serious, at the time it was a frightening experience and left me with a dry throat for days. Arthur Dolphin had top roped this finish before he found the way off to the right, and a year later Paul got me to write it up in the DG new route book. The description in the guide book is too far to the left and underplays the difficulty. Years later I followed the famous American climber Henry Barber up this finish and he thought it warranted E2 which for me in '59 was harder than I was ready for.

A few weeks later me and Roy had a good day on the North Edge of Kinder Scout. We were not to know but it was the last fine day of that amazing summer. We did four new climbs including the first ascent of Jester Crack a 3 star HVS. Another climb, which went unrecorded, was an overhanging off width crack in a corner. Thrutching up the crack looked improbable and devoid of any protection, so I blindly laybacked hoping the edge of the crack would improve but the further I went the more rounded the edge, somehow I stayed on. Sometimes the difference between falling or staying on is by the smallest of margins. From the crag we walked over to Edale. We intended cooking before meeting up with the others in Hathersage but Roy's stove turned out to be broken. There was no shortage of dry dead twigs so we cooked on a fire. That night it rained, it was late autumn and the end of an almost unbroken spell of really good weather that had started at the Easter. It had been the perfect day and would leave a lasting memory of such a good year.

At the time most climbers belonged to a Club, these Clubs were fairly parochial in so much as they often frequented one particular area. Langdale was probably the best example. A previous generation of Langdale lads were people who seemed to be bordering on the criminal with weird nicknames like 'The Moon' and the 'Pale Man'—'The Drake' oddly drowned in Windermere weeks after getting out of jail. Les Brown had left University and gone to work at Windscale the Nuclear plant in west Cumberland where he got friendly with a guy called Pete Turnbull. Pete was from Ambleside and introduced Les to the cream team of the valley. Many of the Langdale lads were not that much older than me but their mentors went back a couple of generations. Men like Bill Birket and Len Muscroft worked in the quarry and became important in the history of Lake District climbing. For the Langdale lads the main requirement for acceptance was either a good sense of humour or eccentricity; climbing came lower down the list. Ackers was small with ginger hair and had a habit when he was pleased of rubbing his hands together and hopping from foot to foot. His regular climbing partner, Roy Warner, was doing his national service and was two years in the Army. This left Ackers short of a climbing partner so for now I filled the bill. He was very enthusiastic. At the time the only thing missing in his life was a girlfriend. He used to reminisce about a girl from Blackpool called the Overhanging Bastion. One night in some doss he rolled on to his back and said with real feeling 'I wish you was a bird.' He was not gay, it was just that the randy little sod needed a climbing dolly bird. Sometimes on a climb he was gripped beyond reason, other times he would climb well but no matter what kind of situation he found himself in he always had enough bottle to give it his best shot. He also possessed a van. It could only climb steep hills in reverse which left passengers pushing but it was transport and safer than riding pillion on a motorbike. During this time I did not see much of my Alpha club mates other than Les. We still met on a Wednesday night but for now this was becoming a thing of the past. Brayshaw had not been out climbing much but turned up expecting the usual gathering and discovered that the previous weekend, Ackers, Mick Burke and me had climbed the Corner on Clogwyn Du'r Arddu and Cenotaph Corner in Llanberis Pass. The autumn before, for some inexplicable reason, Bob had retreated from Cenotaph Corner but a few weeks later did an early ascent of Vember with a seventeen-year old Paul Nunn. By the following summer Bob wrongly concluded that he was not keeping up with the rest of us which his competitive nature could not handle. We never saw him again, it was a great shame. When we had first met him he was using machine nuts with their thread filed out and a nylon sling threaded through for use as runners. Many people over the years have laid claim to this innovation but before joining our group Bob had been Ron Moseley's apprentice with the Rock and Ice Club and the idea for using nuts was probably Moseley's. This development was one of the greatest innovations of climbing history and led to the kind of protection we now take for granted. It is worth adding that nylon rope with its amazing property of elasticity was an even greater one. In the days before nylon when hemp rope was the norm it was said that the leader should never fall. When it was new, hemp rope did have a small amount of elasticity, but very often, not sufficient to allow a second to withstand the pain of rope burns without leaving go of the rope. The leader being tied to the end of a thin almost static rope with a bowline would also find the experience painful. This would be contingent on the rope not breaking, which it often did. However in '58 I did hold Al Parker on a leader fall when he fell off a new route and shot past me the distance he had been above me. We were using full weight hemp that we had bought for our visit to Skye the previous summer. Neither of us was hurt, just a bit sore. A comparison between hemp and nylon rope is illustrated by a fall I took in '69. Me and Paul 'Tut' Braithwaite were doing the second ascent of a climb on Craig Gogarth called T-Rex. Most of the climb was successfully behind us with only a top pitch to do. This pitch is no longer described in the guide book — presumably on account of it not being worth the risk. Tut had taken a belay on two nuts perched in the top of adjacent cracks. I led through and clipped a piton on Dream of White Horse's traverse before heading up the horrible steep grot above. A large flake provided a dubious runner before I had to climb past a shallow cave and a kind of mud stalagmite. I was wet from a drip on the previous stance. Feet below the top and with only one move to go, I was freezing cold, scared and bursting for a brew. I discounted an obvious jam for my left hand—the crack looked crumbly—so instead I pulled on a small flake. It pulled off, slowly. 300 ft below the waves were crashing against the cliff and neither of us liked cold water. As I flew past Tut, the large dodgy flake followed me, narrowly missing my head. Then I stopped like a toy bear on an elastic cord. Tut told me years later, the nuts had popped out and once he had taken my weight he popped them back in. Sounds unlikely but he seldom bullshits. Our saviour had been the new rope and the peg I had clipped on the Dream traverse which had pulled Tut upward, not down and out. Apart from a few nuts our basic rope work was not any different from thirty earlier—the difference was the stretch of the nylon rope. Not in the least bit injured I swarmed back up feeling stupid; the hand jam on the last move was fine.

Hugh Banner had stressed to us the importance of having your own transport, he reasoned that being able to go when and where you want, with who ever, gives you independence. This empowerment would reflect on the quality and amount of climbing you could get done. I chose instead to go to the Alps and anyway. I would have been useless riding a motorbike.

# 5

## FIRST ALPINE VISIT

The train from Paris passed through Cluses at first light. Above huge Limestone towers and big rock faces were emerging from the shadows on either side of the valley. Then in the first rays of dawn we saw Mont Blanc, still mostly in the shadow of the fading night but with her summit catching the early sun, 15000 ft above us. As we got out of the train in Chamonix we met two English lads who were waiting for the train home. One of them had three pairs of symmetrical holes down his face. They were healing up but were tinged in a dark violet stuff, an antiseptic called Gentian Violet. His mate had fallen on him, crampon first, a week before. Welcome to the Alps. Before arriving in Chamonix we had changed trains at Le Fayet. A smaller train runs from Le Fayet to Martigny in Switzerland. Made in the very early nineteen hundreds in its day it must have been the equal of the Mont Blanc tunnel. The road at the time the railway was made would have been little more than a cart track and Chamonix a hidden Shangri-La. To me and Stan Goodwin in 1960, that was how it still appeared. The village itself was fairly small and most of the buildings were built of stone. Many of them had small verandas with wrought iron balustrades. The centre of the village had an air of aging opulence. The rest of the valley was farmed with just a few hamlets like Les Houches and La Praz. The houses in these hamlets were built of wood, with roofs and walls of massive proportions made to hold the weight of huge amounts of winter snow and to last for centuries. The railway station was a grand

AIGUILLE DU DRU – FROM NEAR MONTENVERS

affair and spoke of a genteel pre-war world of rich visitors. It was now fifteen years after the end of the War and the working classes of western Europe had started to have more holidays and money than they had previously experienced. British working class climbers had also appeared. This was a mixed blessing for the locals.

Stan had arranged to meet Andy and I was meeting up with Ackers but first we had to find the campsite. We crossed over the railway line on a bridge that swayed. Not far beyond the bridge was the Biolay campsite. Both sides of the Chamonix valley rise very steeply and are covered in trees. At the time, this forest was still in a pristine state and many of the trees were huge. The campsite was not organized, had no toilets and only a water trough but it was free. Between the trees there were nice grassy spaces. The trees climbed steeply up the side of the valley and the first few hundred feet were used as a toilet. As well as being free the site was very near to town. We were also corralled into one place which was great for socializing. Some of the lads did some weird things. Ken Podmore was a fitter from Stoke, he got really enthused by the grasshoppers and decided to take some home to show his mum. A match box with two or three would have done fine, but Ken got a jam jar and squashed it full. We chose as our first climb a small rock route; the West face of the Albert described in the guide book: *'A short vertical climb of 700 ft high, a suitable exercise when higher peaks are in bad condition, or for practice in artificial climbing. The climb is sustained, graded ED inf in the Vallot Guide. And all the pitons are in place.'* This would be a perfect climb for bullshitting about and with very little discomfort, hardly any bigger than Cloggy but full of pegs. We spent the night in the Chalet Austria, an old peasant building about one mile to the west of the Montenvers railway terminal. It was rough, free and weather tight. About dawn we heard some English people passing by on the path... where did they sleep and were they after the same climb as us? They got there first, three of them, sack hauling three framed rucksacks. They let us pass.

Two small sections of the climb were climbed using pitons and wooden wedges left there from the first ascent years before. Ackers chose to lead these two pitches thinking of himself an expert aid climber having visited the Dolomites the year before. I was instructed to lead the cracks, being in his words a gritstone climber. That was how he delegated our different roles. The second section of aid climbing was the last pitch of the climb. The weather had been overcast all day but with no wind, mist had descended and Ackers was nearly out of my sight. He often panicked but this time he excelled himself. 'The next peg, its fucking twelve feet away' it was only about four feet away but the mist was playing tricks with his imagination. Although he panicked Ackers never totally lost his bottle. Swinging about on a peg his left hand snapped shut with cramp and would not open. With his weight taken on the old piton he could use his right hand to prize the fingers of his left hand open, it immediately snapped back shut. After a rest and with both of his hands working he clawed his way to the top. The descent was easy, but it was approaching dark as we found the path back to the Chalet Austria. The cloud had lifted and we could just see the other three reach the top. The next time we met them they were planning to do the third British ascent of the West Face of the Dru. The leader of the three was a very good climber but pushy. He was killed two years later on the north face of the Eiger. Quite a lot of good up and coming climbers do a few good routes and then hubris makes them too ambitious too soon. As Aristotle advised, there is a fine line between courage and fool hardiness, for now I never had any trouble with that problem lacking either. After two more routes of a similar size to the Albert we were talked into trying some mountaineering.

The Mer de Glace in 1960 was a far larger glacier than it is

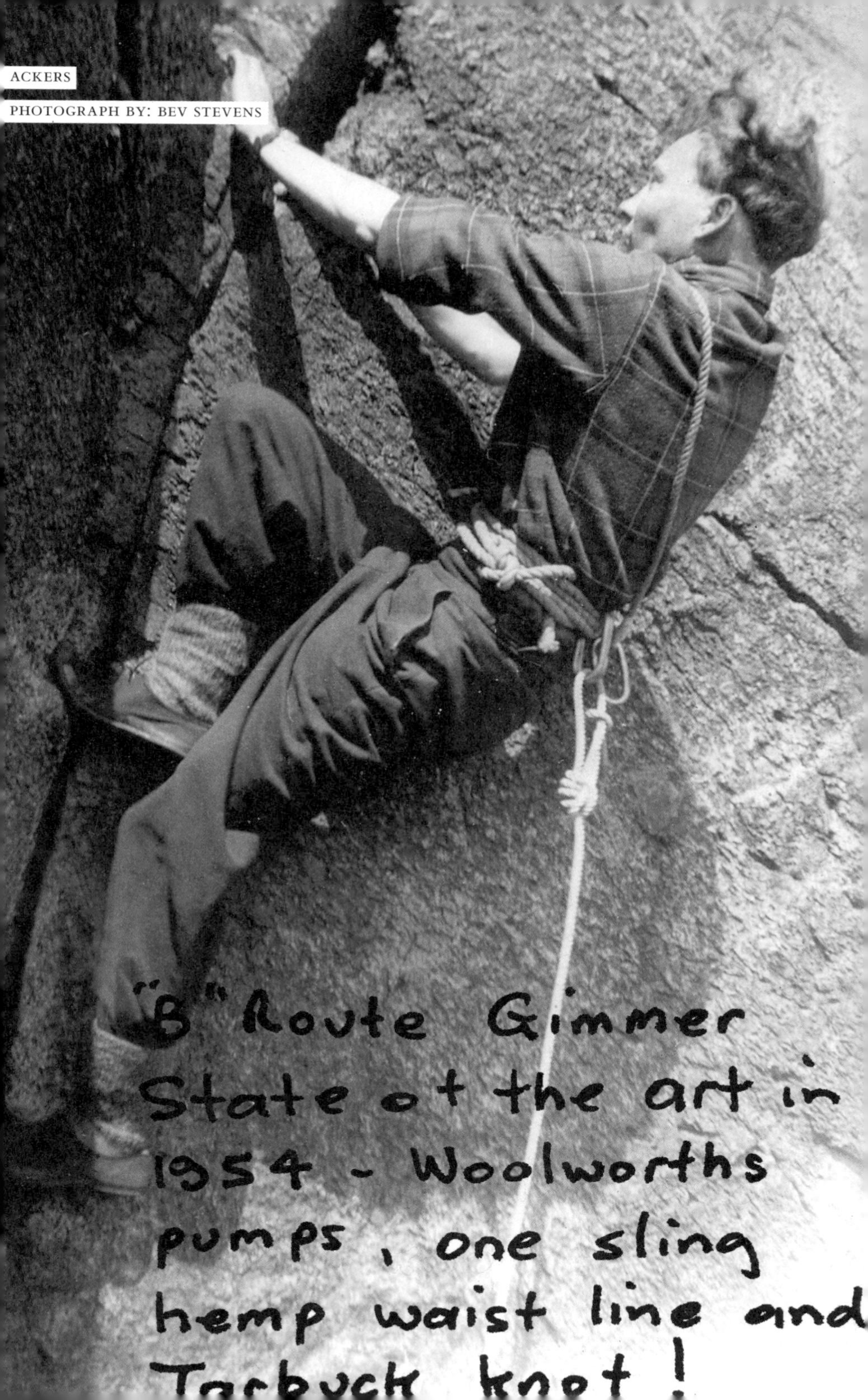
"B" Route Gimmer
State of the art in
1954 - Woolworths
pumps, one sling
hemp waist line and
Tarbuck knot !

ACKERS

PHOTOGRAPH BY: BEV STEVENS

today; no moraine covered its surface, just a wide expanse of blue-white ice. The ladders which then led down to the glacier were getting on for a mile upstream from Montenvers. At the bottom of the ladders was a clean ledge leading onto a small lateral moraine. Just above this ledge was painted a big white square to mark the start of the ladders, for alpinist coming down the glacier. Today this same white square, now hardly visible, is 500 ft or 600 ft above where it was then, the ice has retreated so much. In 2010 the ice of the Glacier under Montenvers hardly shows, so covered in rubble it appears an entirely different place, and even the Aiguille du Dru which overlooks the scene has broken in half.

Two Geordie friends, John Cheesmond and Frank Carrol had talked us into trying the East Face of the Grepon, it is described in the guide as 'A *magnificent climb one of the very great classics of the Mont Blanc range. It is very safe, well protected, and on excellent rock, Height 2600 ft from the rimaye, grade Difficile.*' Two other friends, Geoff Allison and Martin Boysen were intent on trying the South ridge of the Crocodile. Both climbs started from the Envers des Aiguilles Refuge. The way to the Refuge led at first up the Mer de Glace. This was our first time on a glacier. The path to the hut left from the right side of the glacier after a mile or so. We kept near the edge, which was a mistake we should have gone more to the middle. The six of us found ourselves among huge crevasses many of them going parallel to the side of the glacier which meant that we were often balancing along narrow ridges between blue / green gaping holes of unknown depth. I snapped first and put crampons on, sick of playing chicken. At the Refuge there was only one other visitor and the warden. The visitor was an American, probably a hot shot as he seldom spoke, unusual for an American. The weather was bad. After four days in the hut we had no food and only a few re-used tea bags, we were all weak with hunger. Instead of looking at pictures of women in the Refuges stock of magazines, we were staring at pictures of fridges full of food. Bad weather or not, we set out for our respective routes. About a third of the way up the face we got lost in a sea of granite and with snow gently falling we argued the toss as to where the route went. The description in the book mentioned ridges and squat towers, in the mist these could have been anywhere. John Cheesmond led a hard unprotected pitch onto the top of one of the squat towers. With not a piton in site we were lost and for the moment stuck. Down climbing a few feet we found a good piton placement and started our abseil descent. On the descent I got religious and implored God to save us promising that once safely home I would get married, work moderately hard and never push my luck again. After several nights in the pub all was forgotten. On the channel ferry home John, Frank and myself, cooked a meal out on the deck, nobody turned a hair and none of the ship's crew told us to stop cooking. We were just three scruffy looking buggers who couldn't afford the café; changed days.

TRE CIME DI LAVAREDO GROUP—DOLOMITES

# 6

## DOLOMITES '61

The evening streets of Bolzano were deathly quiet. The five of us sat outside a bar drinking coffee, it had been a hard journey with us all squeezed in Bev Stevens' old car. We would finish the journey in the morning. Harry Swales was a ships engineer in the merchant navy and was well travelled. Bolzano had been called Bozen prior to the Great War and had been part of Austria. According to Harry the reason for the deserted streets was fear of the bombing campaign being waged by Austrian terrorists trying to get their South Tyrol back. For now we believed him. The next morning fear took on a more valid meaning as we gazed at the huge rock walls of the Dolomites. The basic colour of the rock is grey but most of the steepest walls are yellow, sometimes there are red streaks which usually denote very loose rock, other times there are black streaks that are usually very sound but often wet. These massive faces have no obvious lines of weakness and at first sight look impossible to climb. That the early pioneers made difficult ascents with very rudimentary equipment is really amazing. The space between each of the bare jagged peaks is stony with some grassy patches — very different from the big glaciated peaks of the western Alps. We camped for free near the Lavaredo hut, which is on the south side of the Tre Cime di Lavaredo group. Soon lots of other Brits appeared. Some we already knew but a group from Sheffield University appeared whom we didn't. For Paul, meeting these lads was fortuitous he had just left school and had a place at Sheffield University starting soon after our return. The lady running the refuge insisted on calling me Piccolissima Bambino and Phil Gordon, Grande Bambino, we must have had baby faces. Graham and Melda Evans had a large frame tent with 3 feet walls, it became the cooking tent. Ackers had an overwhelming ambition to do the Comici route on the Cima Grande, in fact he had thought of nothing else since seeing a lecture about the climb ten years before. On the descent from our first climb we made a mistake in route finding and had to abseil 120 ft into a gully, one hundred feet of it free. This was about ten years before proper sit harnesses were on the market. A make shift harness would be made by wrapping a sling around the stomach and legs, the rope was then run through a karabiner and over one shoulder. The rope only just reached the bed of a gully. Paul went first. I looked at the rusty old piton that we were trusting our lives to and launched in to space, hoping to get down before the piton pulled out. Going too fast to slow down, the rope burned a groove in my neck, for every subsequent abseil for the rest of the holiday I had to use the wrong shoulder. Our next lesson was the excessive time it takes to climb as a three. Bringing two seconds up at once with a waist belay was not an option, especially when belayed to pre-war pitons. So the Demuth Arête on the Cima Ovest took us all day and in the gathering gloom of an approaching storm and with night falling we again took the wrong descent. We got trapped in a gully in the pitch dark and it started raining hard. Ackers had read about climbers drowning in similar situations. He did not keep this information secret and, panic struck, thought me and Paul needed to know. It was an obvious possibility but best left unsaid. After three more routes it was time to do the Comici route on the Cima Grande, luckily Ackers teamed up with another guy, Barry Webb, and we did the climb separately. The Yellow Edge on the Cima Piccola we had found very exposed but the first half of the Comici route is gently overhanging for about 600 ft, at one stage we had to wait about an hour until two lads in front disentangled themselves

CIMA GRANDE – CIMA PICCOLA – PUNTA FRIDA – CIMA PICCOLISSIMA

PHOTOGRAPH BY: BILL BOWKER

EV STEVENS, HARRY 'HANDSOME' SWALES, MYSELF AND PAUL NUNN, ON ROUTE TO DOLOMITES, 1961

PHOTOGRAPH BY: ACKERS ATKINSON

from their ropes that were in an impossible tangle. Waiting about freezing cold, sitting on a little ledge with the sun out of reach we had a pee which landed a good hundred foot out from the foot of the face. A few days later Ackers and Barry set out for the Comici route very early but were still not back until well after dark. When they at last stumbled into the hut we had to carry Ackers to the tent. Suddenly he screamed in agony, his body convulsed with cramp. The tent had no sewn in ground sheet so we lifted the side wall and rolled him out into the night. In his present state he might find food impossible to eat so we pounced on the stew we were warming up for him. Ackers did not mind, he had achieved everything he had ever dreamed of as a climber. Poor navigation on the way home had us crossing France in the middle of the night. Torch lights waving and men with guns, it was a Police road block. The Algerian war following the failed Vietnam War, which had left Vietnam partitioned into north and south had turned France very paranoid. Five young men stuffed in an old car full of gear, the floor covered in stolen apples and in the middle of the night had to be suspicious. Ackers had been driving and as he wound the window down his voice turned to a frightened croak as a sub-machine gun pushed its way in. They soon waved us on our way, another night without a shooting they were probably bored and cold. Bev and Ackers got the car back to their home in Blackpool and while they were in a chip shop the suspension collapsed.

# 7

## FLEISHBANK AND THE KAISERGEBIRGE 1962

This was Herman Bhul's early playground. Aschenbrenner, Rebitsch, Hans Dulfer and many more famous Austrian and German climbers of yesteryear had all cut their teeth here. As already mentioned in the winter of '57 Pete Bamfield borrowed a copy of Hermans iconic autobiography, *Nanga Parbat Pilgrimage*, from the public library. After we had got into our sleeping bags in whatever doss we happened to be in on a Friday and Saturday night, Pete would read the book out loud so we all got the message. The next day we would struggle up some easy route on Kinder or Stanage Edge and imagine ourselves progressing to epics and events such as Bhul describes. Five years later Jim Teasdale and myself stood at the foot of the East face of the Fleishbank in the sleet and rain. The year before I had been in the Dolomites and although the climbs had great exposure and a generally scary atmosphere, with plenty of people about it somehow felt a bit less serious. Now it was late May, midweek with nobody about. Our proposed climb was first done in 1914 by Hans Dulfer. It included two pitches that involved using the rope for tension or a nearly horizontal abseil. Without a belay device or a proper harness these were dodgy manoeuvres, and were made a lot harder by the polished wet limestone. After the second one of these traverses I lost concentration and got off route and had to climb a steep wet chimney. After a strenuous and unprotected fight I arrived at the belay soaking wet and with nervous energy wearing thin. Nonetheless as I brought Jim up the pitch I felt relief. Soon we would join the north ridge and find the summit. The descent should be easy, and before dark we would be back at the tent and a beer in Greisenalm. Above us there was a constant roaring noise, although where we were, there was just an eerie silence. The rain had turned to snow and was sticking to the rock. When we did arrive on the ridge, the snow was in some places waist deep, in others just an icy coating over the rock. The east face had been out of the wind, the ridge was in the full force of a gale. Scrambling up the ridge over the icy snow covered rock was hard enough but with the gale force wind tearing at our bodies it was horrible. Jim's big mountain boots were not the only difference in our equipment. He had moleskin breeches, wool shirt and a ventile anorak. I was travelling light, thin needle cord breeches, light weight boots, small socks and a thin shirt and pullover. My nylon jacket and over trousers had stayed in my sack until the end of the climb. Trying to cope with the wet rock I needed all the friction my clothes could offer, and a nylon suit offered none. After several hundred feet and with almost zero visibility the statue of the Virgin Mary appeared; we had found the summit. Finding the correct descent in these conditions would be impossible. Our only option was to sit down beside the Virgin and hope for forgiveness. By the dawn the wind and snow had stopped the cloud had ascended above the summits but it was very cold. I had stopped the uncontrollable shivering of the night. A lack of a shivering response is an indicator of someone becoming severely hypothermic. On the descent I was often stupidly reckless — another sign of acute hypothermia. Back safely at the tent my hands and toes had become white and a bit numb.

Soon after this mini-epic we left for Chamonix. Over the next ten years the toll road to Greisanalm was surfaced, a lot of car parks made, the business making perfume from pine needles and other links to the past were cut. Over the course of the years I returned to the Fleishbank another three times, always in the sun. It is a good place to stop on the way to the Dolomites but it sadly lacks the magic of the place that captivated me on my first visit.

THE GRAND CAPUCIN, CHAMONIX

PHOTOGRAPH BY: LES BROWN

# 8

## GRAND CAPUCIN AND THE NORTH RIDGE OF THE PEIGNE

When we arrived in Chamonix from a wet Kaisergebirge the weather was settled and good and the Biolay campsite was dry and pleasant. A friend of Jim's from Durham, Brian Snowden, had arrived on his first visit to the Alps, so I went off with him to climb a nice combination of two easily accessible routes. La Brioche and the NN East ridge of the Aiguille 'M'. It was nearly dark when we got back down to the campsite, there was a note stuck to my tent 'Get your gear ready we are going to the Grand Cap in the morning, Les.' No discussion just a plan. I was all set for the pub, one route a week was all my enthusiasm could normally muster and now this. Les Brown had got Paul Nunn and Blonde Rodney involved in the plan. Not knowing what to expect I packed no crampons, little food and only my light weight boots. The Midi cable car felt like a tumbrel carrying us to the Guillotine. The rock summit of the Aiguille du Midi has been hollowed out inside, all nice and safe with café's etc. and then you pop out of a hole and down a snow arête with a drop of seven thousand foot into the valley on the left and on the right side a smaller drop into the icy white waste of the Valley Blanche, a huge snow covered glacier basin surrounded by rock and ice faces, some of which are 3000 ft high. The Grand Cap is a magnificent granite obelisk, up near the top end of the basin, very remote and in the early evening eerily silent. Then a half familiar sound disturbed the silence, Scots voices. One of them had fallen and sprained his ankle; shadows were growing longer as the sun slipped further west around the other side of Mont Blanc. They fortunately refused any English help and made slow progress downhill. We put the rope on in order to cross the bergshrund with Les in the lead. He was emphasizing the need to keep your feet apart in soft snow, so that one foothold did not collapse into the one directly underneath; then he fell. Heading rapidly toward the gaping hole he did a very impressive ice axe brake. The year before, he had been a part of a team that did the first ascent of Nuptse, a giant of a peak adjacent to Everest. We prepared our bivouac on some good ledges below the climb. Above us was a fiercely overhanging wall of wonderful golden granite. Walter Bonatti and Luciano Ghigo made the first ascent in 1951. Much of the climb used pitons and at the time would have been impossible without. After hundreds of ascents, Bonatti's wonderful creation up that face of golden granite had become a porcupine of rusty pitons (Using bolts for protection and using rock shoes, sit harnesses, and belay plates there are now a lot of very difficult climbs up this wonderful spire). The next day we pulled and swung on every piton as we made our way up the wall except at one point. I had left my étriers under an overhang and lay backed a crack, above was a blank wall with vertical flutings which made possible some tenuous bridging. With only one karabiner left which I was saving for the belay, my last runner was down below the overhang and I desperately needed a rest. I clipped a piton and got Les to give me a tight rope after which I moved up to a sloping niche to belay. Now with no karabiners I had to untie and thread the rope through a piton and tie back on, all the time dreading that I might drop the rope. The piton that I had rested on came out when Les pulled on it.

Underneath the summit cowl we prepared to bivi on a small ledge. A large flat stone covered most of the ledge with only about eighteen inches of the underlying ledge exposed. Les insisted on us lying in our polythene bag without being tied into the belay. In the night he rolled off the stone and onto the very edge of the ledge. In the same poly bag, I was about to follow him into space. Whispering and gently nudging him he woke up and then agreed to tie on. Lots of us had these poly bags, although they sweated a lot they were waterproof but too heavy. On our descent we had to go through the Geant ice fall on our way down to the Requin hut. The other three did not bother with a rope and virtually ran. With no crampons I spent ages chopping steps wishing I was tied onto the French teams nearby. By the time I got to the hut the lads were onto their 3rd brew. I learned a lot from this trip, principally that British climbers are immune from falling into crevasses and don't need to rope up on a glacier. I was so chuffed at having got down in one piece that I spent the next week pissed and got on the wrong side of the police. The chief of police had a gorgeous interpreter and through her he established that I was not bad but just an idiot. He lectured me on respect, dress sense and hygiene and hurried me out. Nat Allens wife Tinsel gave me a haircut and a shave and then back to the National Bar.

The sunny hot weather continued, we took it for granted without realizing that it was unusual and spent day after day in the Plage. At the time the Plage was a small, dark green, outdoor lake surrounded by Bridget Bardot lookalikes sunbathing. Most of us had modest ambitions for our mountaineering and usually had an aversion to discomfort and fear. The occasional climb coupled with a magnificent view of the mountains made us more than happy. A few weeks before, I had been on the point of dying with hypothermia in the Kaisergebirge which was quickly followed by the Capucin adventure. Back safely in the valley my mind was full of images. There was the silence of the upper valley Blanche, the glare and heat of the sun magnified by being reflected off so much snow and the effects of altitude. All of which had seemed to make me more anxious. At the tent the homely sound of a primus stove boiling water for a brew, Maurice Simond happily serving

BIVI ON THE GRAND CAP WITH A POLY BAG, 1962

PHOTOGRAPH BY: LES BROWN

PAUL NUNN CLIMBING THE GRAND CAP, 1962

PHOTOGRAPH BY: LES BROWN

us beer in the National bar, even the sound of rain on the fly sheet could sound good and then Nev Crowther and Syd Clarke got bored with all the sun bathing and decided to attempt the north ridge of the Aiguille du Peigne. In fairness it was a modest idea and afterward could be safely viewed from the Plage. Me and Al Parker dragged ourselves from the valley and went with them. We slept by a small lake above Plan des Aiguille and got off fairly early leaving behind sleeping bags and a stack of food for the following night. At the time it was usual to ascend a buttress of snow and rock which led to a perfect 170 m diedre which according to the guide book gave very good climbing. Al led off up the first pitch of the diedre but half way up he took his weight on an old wooden wedge and had a smoke. Above the climbing was as good as the guide book made it out to be and after Al had had a fag we climbed fast and confidently and were soon on the summit. It was difficult to relax on the narrow wedge-like summit so we abseiled down to a massive ledge to wait for Nev and Sid. They arrived and shared some grub, none of us had a watch so we sat about all afternoon on the ledge talking and enjoying the view. Eventually we had to begin a race with the setting sun. Only Nev got back down to the lake, where he then had all the food and four sleeping bags to himself. We spent the night sitting on a ledge smoking Al's remaining fags. When daylight came we were only a hundred feet of easy scrambling above the floor. In the days left to us before we set off home we could look up to the Aiguille du Peigne with pleasure and reflect on a trip that had very little in the way of discomfort or fear.

On our return to the valley two lads from Blackburn had arrived on the Biolay. Before coming out to the Alps they had scarcely climbed anywhere but the gritstone crags near where they lived. From the Dolomites to Chamonix they had done some good quality routes. Brian Bowker was the more experienced of the two and because of their easy going attitude to speed Nat Allen had christened him Bivouac Bill. The name stuck. We arranged to meet up with him in Keswick when we all got home. Bill and his mate Dick had seemed to spend their time either in the hills or cooking potato cakes and drinking stewed tea. The famous American climber, Gary Hemming became fascinated with them and struck up a friendship with Bill.

# 9

## KESWICK

We got into some digs in Keswick and spent the autumn working, eating, and falling in love, drinking and playing darts. It was a sunny warm autumn but the only climbing we did was when we had a visit from Gary Hemming. He had been fascinated by the English climbers he had met in Chamonix, his image of an Englishman was a posh type in a bowler hat. On his way to Keswick Gary called in at Bill's mother's house in Blackburn, expecting Bill to be a one off he found a town full of people in flat hats eating fish, chips and potato cakes. By the end of October Al went home and Bill went down to Wales to work as a voluntary instructor at the National outdoor centre, Plas-y-Brenin. I got a job at Honnister slate quarry for six weeks before I too headed home. Those six weeks were a great experience. The men were hard, basically good but tough. A lorry picked most of us up by the Moot hall in Keswick. I would hear the sound of clogs on the cobbles, then out of the dark they would appear, no conversation just the odd grunt and at various places down Borrowdale the lorry would stop to pick up others, another grunt instead of hello they would take their own very specific place on a plank or the tail board. The younger men had a game which involved throwing stones at each other's shins. The only rule, like in a game of cricket, the stone had to bounce once before hitting the stumps which in this case was their shins. Jumping up and down like buggery to avoid injury, it never got bad tempered, pain was just a part of their everyday life. I had a really boring job working a guillotine; the man who taught me the job assured me the slate dust was harmless. Cynically, I asked him how he knew this; the management had apparently assured them all that it was. A week after I left, the quarry had to close for several months because of the big freeze of '62 / '63 and many of them never returned. Years later Tut was talking to one of the Honister men in the Scafell Hotel. Jacko - reminiscing about me said, 'He's alright Richard but he's a soft ★★★★.'

In Derbyshire that winter of '63 there was voluminous amounts of snow which led to the deaths of two major players in the new route scene — Gray West and Mick Roberts, killed in an avalanche in Chew Valley almost within greater Manchester. They were on a mission to take food to an old couple who lived in a very remote house by a reservoir on top of the moors. The house has long since gone. Gray West produced the first guide book to Derbyshire limestone. I have a copy which I am willing to sell for the right price.

# IO

## BROKEN HEAD

By 1963 motorbikes were going out of vogue with us. They had been a bad mode of transport. Mile after mile, often in the dark and rain, left you cold, wet and knackered. Vans you can sleep in, stay dry and as a consequence get a lot more done. That summer I did a lot of good climbing with one of the Alpha gang, Andy Garvey. He had a van and would second anything I could lead. Although he was a cleanliness fanatic we got on OK With regular decent work and every weekend off my standard of climbing went up. This should have been a good template for how to get the most out of life, but it would be another three years before I would realize this lesson. Instead I gave up my job again and went to the Alps, where four weeks of rain and sleet made me wish I had kept with the regular work script. After a couple of routes the bad weather meant us spending more time in bars to get away from soaking wet tents. Going into the wrong nightclub got us all involved in a fight. The higher echelons of the French climbing fraternity were anything but fraternal in those days. They were, I think, elitist upper class Parisians and we crossed all the boxes for them to take exception to. English working class. Their cultured back ground did not preclude them from all out war and the use of broken bottles seemed to come naturally to them. Out gunned we soon fled but by then the bar was wrecked. We spent the next week trying to avoid the Surete — who probably due to the Algerian war outnumbered the ordinary police. However French justice eventually proved even handed and in the autumn our passports were returned on delivery of a small fine and token damages. In the autumn before starting work I joined Bill and spent nine weeks at the National Outdoor Centre in Wales (Plas-y-Brenin) working as a voluntary instructor. Neither qualifications nor even a proper interview were needed. The centre was like Mervin Peake's book *Gormenghast* in that habits remained unchanged; high tea at five sharp had to be adhered to, no being late off the hill. Dinner at seven sharp, dressed as well as possible. I enjoyed the work but the position was unpaid and uninsured. At the end of October I returned to the real world with only five months to work in order to save enough money for the following summer.

In the spring I would return to the Brenin; the food was free and it would be a cheap way of getting fit for the summer. In the mean time, working at a decent joinery contractors would have been a good idea but the money would have been basic. I chose instead to work concrete shuttering on a site in a chemical plant. The steel structure was about one hundred foot high. The girders had to be encased in concrete and a floor cast every 20 ft. Scaffolding was erected around the outside but the middle of the building was hollow. Walking about on the steel with wooden shutters or Acro jacks was probably more dangerous than erecting the original steel frame but they were paying us for five twelve hour days and four hours for Saturday morning in midwinter. The hours spent in the dark were unproductive and freezing cold and the foreman objected to us lighting fires. The craic with the Irish lads on the job helped the day pass. After work late on Saturday afternoons Maggie; Martin Boysen's girlfriend who was studying for her finals, would give me a lift out to the pub in Derbyshire to meet up with the rest of the Alpha gang. Martin who never seemed to stay in studying still got his degree. By now some of the lads had acquired girlfriends and would spend these winter Sundays festering about walking along the river Derwent. Before Easter

BREDA ARKLESS NEE O-BOYLE, WITH ME ON OCHRE GROOVE LLANBERIS PASS, 1963

I had saved enough money and went back to Plas-y-Brenin. The first day of a rock climbing course was spent tying knots and aid climbing up a tree full of pitons. On Thursday I had three young girls to take climbing. The sun was on its way west as we walked back across the moor from Craig yr Ogof. The girls were really pleased with themselves. We had done a climb called Outside Edge which is a three star 420 ft Very Difficult, They had been a joy to climb with, chattering away on the good stances, enjoying, even if a bit scared, the many exposed positions which the climb has at a very reasonable standard. The next day I was nearly dead. It was Good Friday 1964 and Llanberis Pass was full of climbers down for the Easter weekend. Bill Bowker was still working at the centre as a temporary instructor he had been there since November '62 after he had left us in Keswick. This lack of a permanent position gave him a small wage but was an insult to a good Alpinist and a very good instructor. His opinion was that we should take the course to a more remote location—after all we could have climbed the day before in an empty Llanberis Pass. He was over ruled but at least I got to instruct the star student of the week. I had plans to take John on a variety of climbs, including cracks, walls and even some loose rock. We called on some of my Alpha club mates down for the Easter weekend, had a brew and left for Carreg Wastad. Going to see them turned out to be a lucky move; Bill knew where they were when later on he needed help. He was taking a girl up a 3 star severe called Crackstone Rib. I intended a climb to its right a heap of choss called Rackstone Crib. The students on the Plas-y-Brenin rock courses were, at the time, not issued with rock boots but were supplied with walking boots. To make a level playing field I also climbed in boots. Near the top of the first pitch I did a long step right, a kind of push onto a bent leg followed by a one legged press up. This move would have been a good one if I had not been pushing my weight onto a loose block. I was about 80 ft up and with only one quarter weight nylon

sling on a spike. John with only four days instruction behind him held my fall but the stretch of the rope flicked the sling off the spike and deposited me on the floor. Four days later I woke up starving hungry in a strange room. Bill had held my head together while my mates got the stretcher and sent for the ambulance. Iain Jones, who some years later made the definitive mountain first aid course, was the Doctor on duty, he and my speedy rescue saved my life.

Being unconscious does not always mean that you don't hear things, you just cannot join in. One Sunday I could hear but not speak as some of the lads, who had called by to see if I was dead yet, were discussing a new crag they had found. Martin Boysen and Barry Ingle had just done Gogarth a first ascent on a previously unknown Craig Gogarth. I was listening into an historical event, the discovery of a crag that proved to be a massive new addition to Welsh climbing. A week or so later I was strong enough for a team of doctors to put my head back together. In the course of the operation I heard one doctor say in a Welsh accent 'He has got Celtic cheek bones' as they compared the good side of my face with the one they were trying to make the same. For a second I was dreading the pain of a return to consciousness or a look in a mirror when I did.

# II

## THE DYLAN YEARS '64 / '65

The National centres relied on untrained and uninsured voluntary instructors and badly paid domestics to do most of the work but I did get food and drink as I recovered. Clothes were in short supply but I got some blood stained slings and Karabiners back. Over the first weeks a bigger problem was getting out in the hills, the doctors were of the opinion that I should have spent more time in hospital. I felt that I had not spent all winter on a building site covered in concrete to lounge about. After badgering the boss I was allowed to accompany a group of girls who were going up Snowdon by way of the PYG track, on condition I took no part in any decisions the instructor might make. Above Glaslyn the Trinity gullies looked a more beguiling proposition than staying with the group so without a bye your leave I left them, hoping to see them on the summit. Half way up Central Trinity I came across a narrowing of the gully with a wet mossy overhang above a small cave. That such an obstacle might occur was obvious but as the reality of my weakened state entered my head I sat down to consider the position that my arrogant mind had got me in. After delaying for ages I carried on climbing and with relief found that the overhang was easy. Recovering my fitness was helped by being two stone lighter. A few weeks later Shaun Williams, one of the temporary instructors, had two free days. We spent them going the long walk half way up Snowdon to Clogwyn Du'r Arddu. It was good to be back on Cloggy, the croak of a raven the sweep of dry grey rock often in shadow but pierced in places by bright sunlight. It was empty, not a person in sight, not a breath of wind and bone dry. We did two climbs one day and two the next. The first two in the shade on the East Buttress, Piggott's route and Chimney Route, and two in the sun on the West Buttress, The Boulder and Red Slab. These two days were marvellous I was chuffed beyond reason. Six weeks after getting out of hospital I led the Grasper E2 5c on Tremadoc, not as big as the Cloggy routes but more strenuous. After this I left the centre, I had no role to play although climbing well I was never asked to continue working. After a time staying in Llanberis pass climbing and festering with a friend Dave Little I went up to the Lake District with Martin and Maggie Boysen for four days. We needed a description to a climb on Esk Buttress, the Central pillar which had had its first ascent not long before by two other members of our Alpha club, Pete Crew and Barry Ingle. Martin knew Chris Bonnington who conveniently lived in Eskdale. It turned out that Chris had already done the route but he came along and did the climb again. We would have happily finished after one climb but the enthusiastic Bonnington had us do two more and in the process took some good photographs.

The following two days we spent on Scafell north east buttress. It was midweek bone dry and with nobody else about it was perfect. Away from the shadow of the crag Maggie sat in the sun and after a few routes we joined her. Some events stay in your memory, the three of us sat in the sun eating plums with sticky fingers, not a care in the world. The next day we got in a cloud burst on Mayday direct and finished the day soaked. A few weeks later I left for the Alps with Arthur Williams and Tony Reilly. Arthur was fairly studious — everything he did was given 100%. His sense of humour was subtle, but not light hearted. Any fear or happiness was muted. Reilly was into photography and deep thought. Arthur brought a girl called Sandra with him. On his part it was not a love affair, but for her it must have been a nightmare; we never camped on a proper site with toilet facilities, I must have seemed like a weirdo with a badly scarred face and Tony Reilly's silence must have wrongly seemed judgemental. Just as there was no light hearted craic neither was there any real discord and with Arthur in broad agreement we kept to the sports plan. Our first climb was the Sud-Ost on the Fleischbank. From the Kaiser we headed over the Brenner Pass and into the Dolomites, from the clean orderly Germanic Austria to the tatty easy going Italy. This is no longer the case but at the time officialdom did not seem to exist on the south side of the Brenner. We were heading for the Tre-Cima and specifically the Cassin route on the Cima Ovest. The route has a long exposed traverse above a line of overhangs, faces north and gets little sun. On the first pitch above the traverse leaning down to unclip an etrier, the piton it was attached to came out in my hand. Arthur struggled for ages before asking me how I had managed to do the move. He did not believe I had forgotten and sadly I probably lost some of his trust. Above the traverse the climbing was not particularly hard, but it was fairly wet and not very well protected. Unlike my time with Ackers and Paul in 1961 we found the descent with ease. The next climb on our list was the Constantini, Apollonio on the Tofana di Rozes. It was a very good climb, not too long and in the sun all day. Near the top the climb ascends a very overhanging chimney at the bottom of which is a good ledge. Years before Les Brown had described this pitch to us all, throwing his arms and legs about with shouts of, 'Take in Trevor.' Thinking Les had been exaggerating now seemed naive. At least the ledge was in the shade and as we nibbled some bread a mouse appeared. Was there a colony living on the ledge or did he or she appear out of nowhere? The chimney turned out to be a really good pitch, bridging from one improbable position to another without ever being too strenuous. The descent was easy, walking from one terrace down to another passing old barbed wire, hundreds of shell casing and all the other detritus of war, a reminder of the

CLIMBING WITH MARTIN BOYSEN BELAYING—MEDUSA WALL, ESK BUTTRESS 1964

PHOTOGRAPH BY: CHRIS BONNINGTON

CLIMBING, CENTRAL PILLAR ESK BUTTRESS 1964

PHOTOGRAPH BY: CHRIS BONNINGTON

part our allies of the time, the Italians, had played fighting the Austrians in the Great War.

We then moved on to the Civetta which is on a different scale to most of the Dolomites. Its huge North West Face is several miles long and at its highest is about 3,500 ft. Unlike a true north face, sun does make an appearance. Nowadays rock climbing is very much about absolute technical difficulty. There are still a lot of extremely bold climbers and mountaineers but the biggest majority of climbers prefer difficulty over danger. Big, loose and badly protected is definitely out of fashion. Standing at the foot of such a huge steep face is daunting, taken pitch by pitch the difficulty may not be excessive but the number of them and the increasing problem of retreat, if needed, can be wearing on your nerves. Heavy rain or snow can turn such a place into a pretty unique kind of prison. Along the foot of the face is the Val Civetta, a kind of huge U-shaped shelf, full of bushes and flowers, before the hillside plunges on down into the valley. We camped near the Col Coldai by a small lake, two English lads, Denny Moorhouse and Nick Halls were camping nearby. Nick had a military bearing, fit and serious, Denny by contrast was as mad as a Hatter. Not long after Denny Moorhouse went on to making excellent climbing gear but for now he and Nick were heavily involved with climbing difficult routes. In the mornings Nick would do a routine of muscle flexing at the side of the Lake. Me and Reilly decided this was some kind of bird like courting ritual and that he fancied Arthur's girlfriend. Sandra was unimpressed. Our first climb at the Civetta was the Carlesso-Menti on the NW face of the Torre di Valgrande in the modern guide book V11+ 500 m. At the time there were so many pitons that protection was better than modern bolt protected climbs and pulling on pegs was normal. We tried our best to free climb what we could. Two German climbers passed us by. They were in big mountain boots and pulling on every peg in sight. Lots of German climbers of the day had big

CIVETTA NORTH WEST FACE

ambitions in the Western Alps and thought this way of climbing was good training. In the process they sullied the memory of previous generations of amazing Eastern Alpine free climbers. To a degree the first ascent of the west Face of the Petit Dru in Chamonix with its large use of aid and with its attendant publicity started the ball rolling. It could be said to have reached its apogee with the 1963 winter ascent of the Sachsenweg on the Cima Grande. It made an impression on me at the time because of the men who made this ascent. Two were joiners and two wood machinists. Being a joiner myself I felt some kind of weird pride in this mutton headed escapade and read all about it. The climb was mostly bolted and took something like seventeen winter days and nights. According to the article I read the four of them practised bivouacking in a fridge in Munich. When we got down from the Carlesso-Menti we went for a beer in the Coldai Hut. A German walker asked us in a terse kind of way how two English Guys with no real mountains to train on could climb such routes. How could we describe 50 ft of Gritstone to him? The mammoth publicity that some climbing exploits was attracting was making the sport more exclusive and men like our walker acquaintance had got an exaggerated idea of what a climber should look like. To him we lacked the necessary physique, charisma and arrogance, or maybe we showed too much humility by even talking to him but whatever, it ruined our beer.

Our next objective was the Andrich Fae on the Punta Civetta grade V1, length 650 m. The climb was good and went well. Somehow we bypassed the crux pitch to the left on good grey but unprotected rock. The top chimneys would have been a nightmare in wet conditions but they were dry and really good. Climbs like the Andrich scatter the dolomites. The nineteen thirties saw so many difficult ascents done with rudimentary equipment and up amazing bold faces with few definite lines of weakness. The Andrich was bigger and lacked the protection our last climb had had. The big climbs had less ascents and the higher the quality of the climbers involved the fewer pitons were left behind. This was an equation that has led to these climbs becoming out of fashion. A book first published in 1998 called *Classic Climbs in the Dolomites* by Annette Kohler and Norbet Memmel does not include these big routes, the emphasis being instead on smaller better protected routes in the sun; an admirable sentiment which in old age I completely identify with but in dismissing such a wealth of big serious routes the very ethos of climbing has been changed. Cold shady places with bad protection make things seem more serious and the voids seem even bigger.

We met Tony Howard and Stan Wroe looking like extras from a Sergio Leone film. Tony Howard is a seriously underrated person in the British climbing world where his exploration in Norway and Jordan has been so important. The first ascent of the Troll wall is an example. They had just done the Solleder route on Monte Civetta, which was our next objective. The Solleder route is technically not very hard but at 3,500 ft is big or even bigger than many western Alpine big walls and would be a death trap in the rain. The first part of the climb is where the harder pitches are found and here there were plenty of pitons. On the top third of the climb we came across very few. With some loose rock and very few peg runners or belay pegs the climb was serious and the correct route was very seldom obvious. It was more than good to arrive on the summit in the setting sun. Not very far down from the summit is the Torrani hut but the warden was away in the valley. Starving hungry we found some old packets of food. Two Italian climbers, the only other occupants of the hut, took the stuff off us and said that only Italians knew how to cook Italian food. Ten minutes later they presented us with a big bowl of Pasta in a tomato sauce. We did another climb at the Civetta near the Vazzoler hut before we headed to the Bregaglia. The Cassin route on the NW Face of the Piz Badile was our next objective. The climb is on perfect granite with plenty of pitons in place, 800 m long but with the overall angle of the face less steep than the Civetta. We started the climb after sleeping under a large boulder. Nowadays the climb traverses onto the face from the bottom of the North ridge, along a horizontal ledge for hundreds of feet thus missing out the bottom third of the climb. Old photographs show a snow field which once covered this area of the face. Our approach was by way of a small glacier. We travelled light and were on the summit in six and a half hours. Near the famous Rebuffat crack we passed two Norwegian climbers sack hauling huge amounts of gear. They already had had one bivouac on the face and were probably heading for one or two more. The choice of climbing like a tortoise is predicated on being equipped for the worst eventuality, or one can travel light and be fast enough to avoid being caught in bad weather. On the first ascent Cassin and his companions, Esposito and Ratti met up with two local activists Molteni and Valsecchi. After two days of appalling weather they fought their way to the top only for Molteni and Valsecchi to die on the

TENSION TRAVERSE SUD OST ROUTE FLEISCHBANK – KAISERGEBIRGE

PHOTOGRAPH BY: BILL BOWKER

AUTHOR AND ARTHUR WILLIAMS – SUMMIT OF FLEISCHBANK

PHOTOGRAPH BY: BILL BOWKER

NORTH EAST FACE OF THE PIZ BADILE

PHOTOGRAPH BY: BILL BOWKER

summit. The very nature of first ascents means that progress has to be slow but in the case of climbs that are well equipped it makes more sense to have a good weather forecast and travel fast and light and enjoy the climbing. We descended down the easy south side to the Gianetti hut rather than abseiling and down climbing the North ridge. In the refuge everyone was being Italian, laughing and filling their faces with food. Arthur and me had some oxo cubes and cadged some bread. This was the downside of travelling light. To get back over to the Swiss side we crossed the Porcellizzo and the Trubinasca passes. The descent from the first pass was down hard snow which was a bit dodgy in our light weight boots and no ice axe, the weather was still perfect. We came across a shepherd's summer shelter, on the table was a loaf of bread and half a bottle of wine. The temptation to help ourselves was spared by the sound of sheep with bells rattling around their necks as they and their old shepherd came up the track from the valley. Above the Sasc Fura Hut we went our different ways, Arthur heading for the tents and myself, back to the boulder under the Badile. Tony was an alpine novice so the North ridge of the Badile was our objective. Tony was to bring some food and was meeting me at the bivi cave. He only brought the bare minimum, the lazy bugger walked all that way with a packet of dried potatoes and four tea bags and by now I was starving. The next day there was only one other team on the route — a young Italian Guide with a middle aged man and wife from Yorkshire. They moved fast and we never quite caught them up until near the Gianetti Hut. They were really chuffed and feeling generous, gave me and Tony what they had left of their food. The next morning the weather was bad so rather than walking back over the two cols we walked down into the Val de Mello and hitch hiked back. Our first lift was with a crazy Italian youth in a bubble car which was mostly glass and smaller than a mini car. Before every blind bend he would cross himself and accelerate. Once on the main road we got a lift in a big car with tinted windows a late middle aged driver and a peroxide blonde; all very Mafia like but they went out of their way to drop us off at the Swiss border. With no passports we just walked through, ropes around our shoulders; we were obviously climbers and they never batted an eyelid. We had one Swiss franc and bought some cheap biscuits. On our way back to England we went through Chamonix. Tony, Arthur and Sandra carried on home, I stayed. My lift and climbing partner disappeared; and it never crossed my selfish mind that the economics of the trip depended on there being four of us to share the expenses. I was still not quite wired up right since breaking my head. The craic on the Biolay campsite was good with plenty of mates in residence, all camped near together along with millions of wasps. Garth would buy a huge catering tin of jam, have his breakfast and then leave it with the lid off for the wasps and then repeat the process the following day. Malcolm Cundy was living exclusively on chocolate biscuits, seemingly in perfect health and Gerry Rogan spent hours admiring himself in a mirror he had tied to a tree. For a final route before heading home Oliver Woolcock, Rod Brown, Mike Richardson and I did the traverse of Aiguille Roc and Grepon. On the descent we were caught in bad weather and had to bivi. This time I regretted travelling light.

Four months earlier, waking up in hospital, I had been less concerned about my realigned head than wasting the summer but now I was on my way home with more than 26,000 ft of sustained alpine rock climbing done. I was very lucky that Dr Iain Jones had been on duty that particular Good Friday. Back in Wales me and Martin Boysen got working in the woods helping chop trees down. Martin managed to stick this work for months working with a Welsh Gypsy and living in a caravan. Luckily after a few weeks I got a job at Plas-y-Brenin as a maintenance man. This was a lot easier than chopping trees down. I would also get to see Rose Preston, a girl I had taken climbing the previous spring. Most of that winter I spent helping to build an artificial ski slope. Sometimes when the centre was short staffed I would get the odd day instructing. Pay as a maintenance person was poor. Rose was paid next to nothing as a domestic, any long term future for the two of us at Plas-y-Brenin was limited and by the following June we had sadly drifted apart. Many of the staff sang protest songs for entertainment, to most of the participants it was skill with a guitar or banjo that mattered more than the morals or politics that Pete Seeger or Joan Baez were trying to impart. I preferred listening to Bob Dylan on an old record player.

In July of '65 I cleared my room and left. Six weeks before this a young graduate Steve Martin, having finished his degree at Cambridge came working as a voluntary instructor for a month before starting real work. His father was happy for Steve to have a month off climbing before starting work in the family firm but that would be that, no more climbing, there was a business to run. With none of his friends available to climb with, working at Plas-y-Brenin would have been marginally better than nothing. We fell on each other like manna from heaven and had some really good evenings climbing, helped by spectacularly good weather. We cooked supper on an upside down electric fire, having left the centre well before dinner. We both had had a brilliant month. For me it broke the routine of centre life and helped to make my mind up to leave Plas-y-Brenin. Working in an outdoor pursuits centre seems very beguiling and although secure and cushy they can be insular places, becoming increasingly difficult to escape from as age or boredom takes its toll. Brian Wright offered me a lift to the Eastern Alps where we did another route on the Fleishbank in the Kaisergebirge. The Rebitsh Speigl route was a good climb, very exposed, fairly hard and a lot less polished than some of its neighbours. For Brian it was either his second or third first British ascent on the crag.

I had made an arrangement to meet Mo Anthoine in the Dolomites. When I found him their tent was pitched near the Vazzoler hut in the midst of long healthy grass and a sign in five languages saying 'No Camping'. The farmer never said anything but would run his cattle past our tents every morning. Mo dropped his piton hammer off our first climb. The hut warden kindly lent us another one, it was engraved Carlesso-Sandri: the names of two famous Italian climbers from the pre-war era. Hopefully it would be a good talisman. The Philipp-Flamm route was our objective – 1050 m grade VI sup and with two short sections of easy aid climbing. Pete Crew and Alan Wright had done the first British ascent three years before. A year later Paul Nunn and Martin Boysen had a nasty time finishing the climb when a rock fall broke Paul's lower leg when they were four pitches from the top. In order to save an hour's walk in the early morning, we slept under a boulder in the Val Civetta. In the night a storm broke turning the face into a three thousand foot waterfall. We bought some bread off the warden of the

77

Tissi hut and spent a second night under the boulder. The following morning was fine but we started up the route already hungry. The middle section of the climb ascends a huge diedre the climbing was good with just sufficient pitons to make it enjoyable. The top of the diedre ends in overhangs but a narrow grey gangway makes a line of weakness across the left wall. This traverse is very exposed with nearly two thousand feet beneath your feet. Pete Crew said he had been sticking line slings to small spikes with chewing gum as he made this traverse. This being the first British ascent no one could say bullshit, so we believed him. Mo spied a piton on the steep wall above the gangway and decided to make a try that way. The piton was in a horizontal flake which turned out to be a straight forward hand traverse. After a lunge Mo reached the piton with his middle finger. The belay peg had probably been there since the first ascent and if he continued dangling about on one finger unable to clip the peg he was looking at a big fall which would have to be held some distance below me. Along with a frantic dialogue he regained control and finished the pitch. A semi aid wall led on to some easy ground and up to the last grade VI pitch. To say it was loose is an understatement, with my hands above a bulge my feet were rotating like a cyclist trying to get some purchase on the loose rock underneath, all the time showering Mo with stones. Relieved at the notional idea that the main difficulty was behind us we looked with horror at the gully that we had to climb for the next few pitches. It was more like a river from the storm two nights before. Once above the gully there was a deep cave which looked secure, so soaking wet we decided to bivouac and like idiots crawled into the ice filled interior. If we had not been so wet we would have had enough time to finish the climb that evening. Inside the cave was bloody freezing and after shivering all night it took us ages to get moving. Two pitches above the cave and only three to go, a storm appeared. Not knowing how long it would last we pressed on. I had to climb a bulge on some pitons followed by a nasty little traverse to arrive in the final gully. Before bringing up Mo I tried to warm my hands, with eyes shut and nearly crying with pain my hands regained circulation and when I opened my eyes the storm had passed. Peaks for miles around were glistening in the sun with a covering of rapidly melting snow. After an easy scramble to the summit we were soon down to the Torrani hut 250 m below the summit. The warden was sitting in the sun talking to the only visitor. We hung our wet clothes on the handrail and having no money to spend looked the other way. The visitor sent two glasses of Grappa over to us. Eventually the three of us set off down, us to the Vazzoler hut and the walker to the valley feeling pissed but very happy. Part of the way down there was a Via Ferrata mainly comprised of exposed ladders, our new friend was very scared and helping him down was decent payment for all the Grappa. Once at the tent I went to collect the sleeping bags from the boulder in the Val Civetta, deviating from the path to buy some milk from the farm. Inside was a huge copper cauldron which had the remains of a wooden fire underneath, the walls and ceiling were black with the smoke of what looked like centuries of use. This was where they made cheese, and by the look of things slept, their belongings stored on a few shelves. I was sold some milk but on the way out I had to squeeze past a massive bull that the children had herded with some malice into the narrow exit. The farm was a glimpse into a bygone world. The next day we left for Chamonix. The two times I had been to the Civetta were forever etched in my memory, it had been truly wonderful.

The view from the Montenvers Hotel used to be dominated by the Aiguille du Dru separated from the observer by what was then the impressive sight of the Mer de Glace half of the peak is still there, but the huge orange south west pillar and most of the west face has gone, swept away in several gigantic rock falls. The Dru was iconic, so often an overused adjective, in this case it almost seems an understatement. The trip on the Montenvers railway was often the first proper sight and access to a glacier for most young British climbers. The Mer de Glace with the upstream skyline of the Grande Jorrasses was awesome but the West face of the Petit Dru, would usually divert most people's gaze. The sight of the Dru is sad today: mountains seem so timeless, but with the Glacier at least 100 m below its 1960 level and the Aiguille de Dru in half, it makes me feel as if my age should be measured in geological time. The west face was climbed first in 1952 using mostly aid and siege tactics, ethics that became almost normal over the following few decades. To the right of the west face there used to be the south west pillar which had its first ascent in 1955 climbed solo over five days by Walter Bonatti. There is this comment in the present Guide book: '*The first ascent of this magnificent rock climb constitutes one of the most remarkable exploits in the history of Alpinism.*'

On my way from the Civetta to Chamonix I had had various adventures. First I met a French hippy who had a haversack full of heroin. He was hitch hiking home from Afghanistan. I got a lift from somewhere near Vicenza all the way to Torino in a car with tinted windows. The driver never spoke until he dropped me off, it was then he told me in good English which bus to take to get me to the Aosta side of the city. I slept among some trees on the central reservation of the Autostrada, it felt safe! The next morning I took a bus to Chamonix. In Aosta I needed a bank to change a traveller's cheque for my ongoing bus fare. The driver showed me the way to the bank and en route found that I came from Manchester. He then started jabbering in broken English about how marvellous Manchester United were... It took us ages and as we walked slowly back to the bus the other passengers were waving and shouting abuse. France was alright but it seemed sad to be leaving Italy.

We had the Bonatti pillar on the Aiguille du Dru as our objective.

Me and Mo had been joined by two friends John Moss and Bill Barker. At the bivi site we met two veterans, Al Hunt and Ron James, who were heading for the west face. Sometime before dawn we were woken by what sounded like cowbells. It was the famous American climbers John Harlin and Royal Robbins going to do a new route. The noise was from the pitons they were carrying, from crack tacks to large Bongs, all completely new to us at the time. A dangerous couloir led up to the start of both the West Face and the Bonatti pillar. Al Hunt and Ron James were heading for the West Face which left the couloir at mid height. Our route went all the way and traversed across the head of the couloir to reach the pillar. It is essential to be under way before first light to avoid rock fall as the morning sun melts the ice that glues the loose rock together. We had overslept and there were now the lights of seventeen separate head torches in the couloir shining like glow worms. With so many climbers in the couloir we had missed the boat and settled back down to wait but by first light there were still three climbers stopped high up in the couloir. One of them had been injured and the other two must have been trying to cajole him into going on. We delayed our start. We had to either go back to the valley or take our chance with the inevitable rock fall. Mo was treating us to a burlesque show. He was wearing pair of women's tights to keep his skinny legs warm, his shoulders were out of proportion to his legs which made him look as if he was assembled out of spare parts. Ron James got pissed off with this and decided that he and Al Hunt were going to start come what may. We followed them, all climbing unroped and taking independent lines. The three climbers above started to climb down and immediately knocked a rock off which hit Ron on his shoulder. Amazingly he did not fall off; both Al Hunt and Mo were climbing right behind him. Al and Ron descended having refused our whispered offer to help them down. The rest of us roped up and started belaying. Near the top of the couloir an enormous rock fall from behind the Pillar swept down, missing the four of us by a whisker. Mo was shouting at God to go and fuck himself. I was scared witless and could only croak to tell him not to blaspheme. At the time nobody wore crash helmets, there were some on the market in Europe but they were pretty useless. The route turned out to be over pegged especially with wooden wedges. This made hand jamming the often perfect cracks awkward. I was watching a parrot shaped rock on the Flammes de Pierre to gauge our progress but we never seemed to get any further away from it until after the 40 metre wall. This vertical blank wall had a thin crack running up it but without even the smallest of foot ledges. Before harnesses were used the rope was tied in a bowline round the waist. Our ropes were not long enough so we would have to take a hanging belay. Dangling from a rusty piton without a harness is painful and scary. This was especially so when Mo had to climb past me to lead through. At that point we were only attached to the rock by two old pegs. Above, the climbing improved and as the sun began to set the temperature became pleasant. Eventually we reached the shoulder and a good bivouac site. The descent went well, but a lack of water gave us all a mad thirst. Back at Montenvers we had to struggle with the tourists to get on the train back to Chamonix but in the melee one of them had left half a juicy pineapple behind on a seat; just great.

The Brown Whillans route on the Aiguille de Blaitiere had its first ascent in 1954. At the time some of the free climbing must have been the hardest in the Mont Blanc area. The fissure Brown is still grade seven and it must have been impossible to aid climb until someone came along with some enormous wooden wedges. For us these wedges were difficult to climb past and gave the impression that they could easily pullout, but at least they made the pitch possible. Above the climbing was superb, sustained but with just enough in situ protection. It was the practice at the time to climb to the Fontaine ledges and avoid the upper pitches. Mo and myself were curious and continued. After a pitch or two came a steep crack with a nasty unprotected layback to start. My right foot slipped off a quartz crystal and only luck prevented me falling on to a rock strewn ledge 30 ft below. The rest of the pitch was really good. Could this pitch have been the mysterious Fissure Fix; years before a climb did exist on this area of the Blaitiere put up by Pierre Allain and Fix in 1947 but it had disappeared from the guide books after the bottom part of the face collapsed. We got down to the campsite well after dark. I had followed the light from the cigarettes Mo was chain smoking, it seems he could see in the dark. I was knackered. The Brown Whillans in its entirety did not have the cachet that the Bonatti Pillar or the Phillip Flam did but although less serious, was harder, a lot more strenuous and arguably had some better climbing. I climbed in big boots and sack, Mo climbed some of the climb in rock boots and carried his boots in his sack, he justified this by having met a bloke on a train who told him a pound on your feet is the same as four pound on your back!

Before going home John Moss and myself did the Frendo Spur on the Aiguilles du Midi and in the process ran into Don Whillans and James Fullalove aka Dan Boon. We all had a very late start and until reaching the ice arête climbed solo. John, Dan and myself climbed in a group going at the same speed, which was as fast as it was possible for us to climb. Whillans was climbing so fast he had disappeared. We found him sat on a big ledge relieved to be alive. To pass the time while we caught him up he had been doing hard variants and on one of his variants had nearly fallen off. His only comment was that it was like Three Pebble Slab on Froggart Edge. Before we moved on he shared some of the food he was carrying with us, an impressive act of generosity. A rock buttress at the top of the climb bars access to the snow ridge which leads easily up and in to the Aiguille du Midi cable car station. A storm a few days previously had covered some of the rock with snow and ice.

ALAN HUNT ABSEILING OFF THE SUMMIT OF THE GREPON 1964
WITHIN THE HOUR WE WERE ALL IN A FULL BLOWN BLIZZARD—PHOTOGRAPH BY: REG PHILLIPS

Whillans seemed to have a moment of doubt. I thought that we should try a different line then at least it increased the chance of one of us reaching the top. Our chosen way started up an overhanging crack followed by a long hand traverse. Don's head appeared from around a corner fifty feet away and on the same level. 'Fight it kid.' He never said that he and Dan were on a climbable line. At the end of our hand traverse was a snowy ledge from which it seemed possible to gain the corner that Don had appeared from. Above this ledge an icy hole seemed to offer an alternative way. Full of hope I squirmed up the hole onto a small ledge of rotten Granite, with no chance of placing a piton I had no belay, I sat with my legs across the hole hoping that if John fell off I could hold him. When he reached the snowy ledge he continued the traverse easily around the corner to where Dan was belayed. Reversing safely down the icy hole was too dangerous to consider so I was stuck. After what seemed ages and with darkness descending a rope came snaking down from above. The wall above me was blank so I climbed the rope, hand over hand. Near the top Whillans growled 'Try using the fucking rock!' The rope went from a belay which was over to one side and was deviated around Don's ankle to enable it to hang vertically down the wall to me. Don was not tied on to any rope, if my weight had pulled his ankle too hard sideways, he would have been in space. We spent a cold but safe night in the Midi cable car station. The toilets had a fan heater just behind the bog and we found a room with a stove and coffee. Dan Boone was a bit of a one off. Three years later he climbed the North face of the Eiger, the Walker Spur on the Grande Jorrasses and the Pear Buttress on the Brenva face of Mont Blanc with Ray College, ('an aging alpinist') in less than a fortnight and then disappeared from the climbing scene.

Once back in Wales I heard that there was a month's pay at Plas-y-Brenin. Having no money I went. The warden asked me, 'Had I left and if so why.'

## 12

## DEATH ON THE BRENVA

1966 The final whistle blew, after 90 gripping minutes England had won the world football cup. The bar was full of Germans, who looked really pissed off, Mo ran around the bar laughing. Nearly a week before we had met an Austrian film director on the cable car as we were coming down from the Torino Hut, he wanted us to work for free, on a climbing film acting as porters. This suited Mo as he needed an excuse for us to stay off the hill as he was determined to see the football match. So we waited, meanwhile the sun shone out of a cloudless metallic blue sky. On the big mountains the isotherme was low and a strong wind blew. The Brenva face of Mont Blanc began to glisten with ice. When the director came for us Mo and Jacky had gone to Aosta for the day so we missed out on being film stars. The day after, we went off up the hill anyway. Getting a weather forecast would have been a good idea, the bivi sac and good gloves an even better one. On our previous foray we had not travelled light, Mo insisted on taking raw potatoes, excess fuel, and being generally kitted out more like marines than alpinists. As we were packing our sacks for the Brenva Face, a word of protest and a suggestion we might travel a bit lighter than our last trip had an exaggerated effect on Mo and everything we might need in bad weather got chucked out of the sacks.

The Col de la Fourche bivi hut is in a remote position on the Frontier ridge of Mont Blanc. We set out late from the valley catching the last cable car to the Col du Geant. The

Valley Blanche is surrounded by large faces of rock and ice, the snow was turning mauve and the shadows going black as the sun began to set on the far side of Mont Blanc. Four years before, I had been overwhelmed by the magnificence and the silence of the place as we ascended to the Grande Capucin from the Aiguille du Midi. Now in what was left of the light we climbed steeply up from the glacier to the hut, we were disappointed to find the place was nearly full. On the bottom bunk were four other Brits. Three Scots and one Geordie, on the top bunk was a cream team of French climbers. The other Brits were pleased to see us; the banter with the French was becoming caustic and they had numbers on their side. Not long after our arrival two Belgium lads appeared, the French now turned the barracking on to them, the pair of them retreated into a corner obviously nervous. They started to melt snow on their stove for a drink and then accidentally they knocked over a large billy can of water that belonged to the French, who went ballistic. This was our last laugh for a long time. The other Brits were in two teams; Jim McCartney, a big Aberdonian, and Colin Spacy, a small Geordie and then Willy McGibbon and Davy Ross, both from Glasgow. We were all going for the Brenva Spur. We never did find out if they set out as two separate teams or if they knew each other before they left the valley. By the time me and Mo stirred ourselves the hut was empty, everyone had gone, too early in our naive opinion and without sufficient sleep. We crossed the Glacier to the Col Moore. The Moon reflected on the snow bathing large areas in light but in the shadow it was pitch black. Above Col Moore the way ahead was mixed snow and rock, easy but dark. Not far above we could hear the other four, they accidently dislodged a large boulder which crashed into a buttress above our heads and broke into small bits, if we had not locked bodies in a panic struck embrace, one or both of us would have been hit. The Glasgow lads had had one of their ropes cut by this falling rock. This shortened rope caused a problem the following day. As dawn broke we climbed up a nice snow arête and were now catching up with the other four. Five or six hundred feet from the top of the climb the snow slopes became hard ice which would have required a lot of unprotected step chopping. Over on the right a possible route was blocked by a wall of seracs, under which was a rock pinnacle where we found the other four. Only one of them wanted to carry on but a descent was not a nice proposition. Jimmy McCartney worked for Hamish MacInnes running ice climbing courses in Glencoe: this serac barrier should not prove an impossible barrier for one us. The first pitch was a twenty foot wall of soft ice, so we sent Jimmy up it with some verbal support. He belayed in an ice cave. Mo was next whilst I brought the others up to me. Lower down on the climb the head of Mo's ice axe had parted from the shaft. He had continued just using the head of his axe in one hand; a few years later he started a business making ice axes with unbreakable fibre glass shafts. Up in the cave Mo and Jimmy knocked the shaft of Mo's broken axe into the hard snow which made a good belay, after which Jimmy traversed a kind of ice foot ledge which led out of site around the corner of the Serac. This traverse was very exposed and being nearly out of earshot it was difficult to communicate with him, so we had no idea if he had reached easy ground or was stuck in the middle of nowhere. Mo brought me up to the cave then he followed Jim. I brought the other three up and then provided them with a back rope as they seconded the traverse. When it was my turn, I had no back rope and nobody was taking my rope in. I had no idea in what kind of horrible situation the others might be. I traversed around the corner expecting the worst and there they were all gathered on easy ground. We ascended good snow slopes to the Col de la Brenva, relieved and very happy. Once on the Col relief turned to fear, the wind was strong and very cold with large hailstones. Visibility on the Col was still clear but above us in the direction of the summit the cloud cover was total and descending rapidly.

The easiest method of descent from the Col is to climb easy ground to the Summit and descend the Bosses ride to the Vallot Bivi hut. The other two ways are either a long traverse to the Col du Midi or a descent of the corridor route. For the first of these alternatives the way leads around the summit of Mont Maudit and then a descent to the Col Maudit, followed by an ascent of Mont Blanc du Tacul and then a descent to the Col du Midi. This descent is a long way and although relatively straight forward in good visibility would be a nightmare in bad weather. The third way would be by the Corridor Route which led straight down from where we were to the Grande Plateau and on down to the Grand Mulet Refuge. Although one of the original routes up Mont Blanc it was no longer used chiefly because of large crevasses running across a slope. In light of later events this might have been the best option if we had been prepared to leave behind sufficient rope to abseil over any obstacles. Colin Spacy and me favoured the way over the main summit to the Vallot hut. We all agreed but a few hundred feet above the Col, the wind became murderous, my hands had gone numb, the gloves I had had long since disintegrated. We all changed our mind in favour of the traverse over to Col Midi. I still think in retrospect that this was a mistake. Conditions would have been extreme going over the summit but with speed and determination it was by far the nearest option, the weather was still not at its worst and we were all going well. Later on that same day some other friends did summit out on that ridge from the Sentinel Rouge climb, and one died on the descent of the Bosses ridge, so I suppose it was not a foregone conclusion that we would have done any better. We were probably earlier than they were with more time left before night fall but in the event we turned around and set off toward Mont Maudit. An easy traverse on the Chamonix side enabled us to avoid going over the summit and we crossed a rocky Breche that led us down onto a steep snow slope where we found a wooden stake hammered into the snow for use as an abseil point over a Bergshrund. The weather was now worse we were engulfed in a complete white out—trying to find the easiest way was impossible. Some distance below the abseil we descended a huge easy angled snow slope. It was loaded with wind slab. It cut perfectly into neat blocks so we constructed a bivouac ledge in the middle of the slope. All of us were completely blasé about avalanches and had no idea how dangerous this slope was becoming. My bivi sack was in the valley; a victim of Mo's purge on weight. Colin had one and the Glasgow lads had one. I got in theirs and Mo went into Colin's. With three people inside the sack breathing was a problem and all night spin drift slid down the slope so that we had to keep on digging ourselves out of the snow. Dave and Willy had taken their boots off and put their legs into their rucksacks. In the morning their boots were buried under four foot of snow. The other three in their struggle to breath had put a rip in Colin's bivi sheet. Next day we carried on down the slope following our noses and out into a snowy Cwm between Mont Maudit and Mont Blanc du Tacul. I was in front convinced the Almighty was showing me the way. The wind had died down in the night but had started again. Now the Glasgow team produced a map and compass, the first we knew they had one. Not having a clue where we were made this useless. Colin voiced this opinion to me. Although this was true he nonetheless seemed a bit defeatist as though his will to survive was decreasing. I put my faith in the Almighty and carried on up the slope. We reached a ridge, down the other side a huge snow slope disappeared into the gloom. We did not know for sure but it was down this slope that the descent from Mont Blanc du Tacul to the Col du Midi went. To our left a ridge disappeared into the cloud, it looked rocky. A descent of the snow slope had been ruled out, vast quantities of new snow spelt potential avalanches which convinced some of the more experienced members of the team that it was a bad idea. I thought it was a risk worth taking. We were all to a greater and lesser degree hypothermic. The weather was by now horrendous any technical manoeuvres other than putting one foot in front of another and attempting to lose height and quickly could definitely spell disaster. Some of the team wanted to stop and bivouac by the rocks, this was mad there was absolutely no shelter from the bitingly cold gale but their will was evaporating. Mo preferred to descend the rocky ridge, but I could not visualize where it could possibly lead at the bottom and where we could get onto easy ground. Abseiling and down climbing would be horribly cold work. It did however have the merit of knowing that we would be going in a straight line downhill. Out on the open snow slope there would be no feature that could be used for direction and in the conditions we could have wandered anywhere. I eventually saw the merit in this and agreed with Mo to descend the ridge. Three of the others sat by a rock intending to bivouac and reluctant to move. Mo, Jimmy and me had no intention of stopping, without our losing altitude and quickly, we were done for. Reluctantly they saw the sense in this and we split into two groups of three and set off down the ridge. In front Mo, Jimmy and Colin were gaining ground on me and the other two. Mo and Jim were sharing the work, setting up abseils, pulling the rope down, retying the rope and down climbing to the next abseil. Behind I found myself doing most of the work. At one point I was down climbing with two ropes around my neck. Going from the bottom of one abseil to a large flake which might make a good anchor for the next abseil I lowered myself down to a small ledge using the flake for my hands. The flake came off, I grabbed wildly, an instinctive desperate lunge, my brain already thinking 'Bastard this is it.' Underneath where the flake had been was a smaller spike, my hands grabbed it and I stopped myself. Lower down Mo and Jimmy had abseiled down a groove on the right flank of the ridge, and Colin was waiting for his turn to descend. From my position several hundred feet above him, he seemed too still and was stood motionless, as if the spark had gone, any will to carry on moving had deserted him; it had. When we got to where Colin had been he had gone down to Jimmy, their abseil rope still in place. Jimmy was shouting Mo's name into the wind but Mo could not hear him. He had continued the abseil and then down climbed to a large snowy ledge in between some rocks and had fallen asleep. I abseiled down to Jimmy, he was attempting to lower Colin down to where he thought Mo was. Colin was losing consciousness, his hands were holding anything they could find to grip onto preventing him from being lowered. I continued my abseil past Jimmy so that I could pull at Colin. The lowering rope was tied around his waist and had pulled his duvet jacket and other clothes up exposing his back, he was brown with the sun and obviously undernourished. He had been out in the Alps all summer and had probably not eaten enough. When he ran out of money he had written home tapping his dad up for a loan; his dad sent him just enough money for the ferry. Colin had used the money in a game of cards which he won, met Jimmy and came up the hill for one last route. Now he was talking to himself about the sun and the warm rock in the south of France; he had just returned from a trip to the Calanque, an area of Limestone inlets famous for its climbing near Marseille. A truly gorgeous place to go when the weather was bad in the Alps or just for fun. The rope that was being used to lower Colin was the rope that had been cut in the rock fall near the start of the route. It was too short. I was still on the abseil rope and had some rope left underneath me. I tied the ends together, clipped one rope into a karabiner on the strap of Colin's rucksack and let him slide down to the knot. Using the rope for my hands I cramponed down, unhooked Colin and held on to him as we slid down to the ledge which Mo was now trying to chop flat with what was left of his ice axe. We all gathered on the ledge, Jimmy and Mo got Colin into the bigger of the two Bivouac sheets and started to try and resuscitate him. After ages of desperate effort it was obvious Colin was dead.

Dave and Willy got into their bivi sheet, sharing it with Jim. Mo and I got into Colin's ripped Bivi sack and started to make a hot drink for us all. In the mountains I had often been in storms but never as bad as this one, it was still raging and would for three more days. Colin was young fit and fairly well equipped. He died at the only sheltered spot we had been in since the onset of the storm, we were all in a bad state and like the rest of us if he had managed for another hour he might well have survived. The next morning it was calm and still very cold, about midday Jimmy shouted to us in his broad Aberdonian accent that the sun was shining. It was but only slightly. Just above us was the Col du Midi, we had descended the ridge too far. We made Colin's body secure and tied his crash helmet in a position to try and make him more visible for the rescue team. One abseil brought us onto a snow slope which we then had to traverse up and across to reach the Col. It was very hard work with the snow waist deep, we took turns breaking trail making a huge perforation in a slope where thousands of tons of unconsolidated snow was likely to avalanche. The weather was closing in again, visibility was decreasing and the wind had returned. Coming up towards us from the Col were two big men, it seemed as if we were all experiencing the same illusion. French Mountain troops were camping on the Col and the two figures were Doctors. They give us some candy bars and we followed them to their camp. A large rectangle had been made of snow blocks about two metres high with a floor area big enough for several tents. A sergeant was just leaving with an armful of small marker flags, we were told to follow him. The soldiers knew the weather was going bad again and these markers were to show the way between their two camps. They had radioed the other camp and we were greeted with hot coffee and half a Baguette each full of pâté and cheese. Not far above us was the Cosmiques refuge, I went a different way from the rest, I had tears in my eyes that I did not want the others to see. We were now safe but I was thinking of Colin, dead so near to salvation. The hut guardian filled a tin bath full of hot water and had us sit with our feet in it. The French Doctors reappeared, they first treated Jimmy's eyes—he had been suffering with snow blindness—and then they rubbed some antiseptic cream on our frost bitten digits. The day after the weather had become so bad the soldiers left their camp and moved into the Hut. We had no money for food but the soldiers would eat their fill of their dinner and slide across the table to us what was left. Mo smoked, so he asked the soldiers for a cig and instead of one they gave him a packet of ten Gauloise. Whenever he looked as if he needed another they gave him another ten. The morning of the third day was wall to wall blue sky, my feet and some of my finger ends were numb, getting boots on was a struggle. The Aiguille du Midi cable car station took us about an hour to reach. Jostled in to a cabin with a lot of tourists, an Italian lady was making a fuss of Jimmy's inflamed eyes, so to divert her attention he held my hand up to show her. I had not noticed but some of my finger ends were changing from gray to black. Down in Chamonix Mo disappeared with a journalist, the others vanished and I went in to the Biolay campsite, where there were a lot of my friends, two of whom gave me a lift through the Mont Blanc tunnel to where Mo, Jackie and myself were camped.

Dr Tom Patey had appeared on the campsite. Tom was the GP in Ullapool in the north of Scotland. He was not only a very good mountaineer but was one of the really great characters of the British climbing world. Tom gave us a letter to take to Doctor Mike Ward at The London Hospital, who had been the Doctor on the first successful Everest expedition in 1953. They had two Hyperbaric Oxygen machines at the hospital, and Tom thought that treatment with this might save us having to have any fingers or toes removed.

Mo, Jackie and myself, being camped on the Italian side of

Mont Blanc had no knowledge of what if any arrangements were made to bring Colin's body down to the valley. Despite our shared ordeal we knew absolutely nothing about the others and had never met them before. In any event, in our present state we would have been unable to be of any help. In 2009 I was on the Inverness climbing wall with a friend Davy Moy reminiscing about old times, it transpired that he had helped to bring Colin's body down off the Hill. Rescue back then was expensive and very few British climbers were insured for what seemed to our minds an unlikely event. Also, the rescue services did not seem to be bothered about a dead body.

There is an excellent and very readable book by Anne Sauvy *Mountain Rescue Chamonix - Mont Blanc* which explains perfectly what was going on. A seminal event was taking place at that exact time, precipitated by a large rescue on the West Face of the Petit Dru, which turned into a complete shambles. The successful rescue was eventually accomplished by an amateur team of climbers, the American Gary Hemming, a friend of mine Mick Burke and the famous French alpinist Rene Desmaison. Anne Sauvy writes '*The continuing shortcomings of the Mountain Rescue Bodies were exposed by these events leading to further organisational changes. The PGHM emerged as the main rescue services in Chamonix.*' Davy told me that a group of British and Irish climbers formed a team, intent on recovering Colin's body themselves; one hurdle to which was the expensive cable car to the Aiguille du Midi. Mr Snell the owner of Snell Sports Chamonix stepped in and paid this expense for everybody. Snell and Maurice Simond (owner of the Bar National) were very good to British climbers, although I suppose we kind of paid our debt to Maurice by spending a lot of our money in his bar. With our hands and feet bandaged Jackie drove us all the way to the London hospital. On the way over the Jura we had a wonderful view of Mont Blanc shining white in an azure blue sky. Mike Ward read Tom's letter and within the hour had us both in hyperbaric machines.

Four weeks later they let me out of hospital. Before going back home I went out to Dagenham to see some relatives, after the experiences of the last two months the visit had a bizarre feel to it, but it helped to expel the horror. My cousin Gordon was big. His nose was small and sharp; his thin lips had the redeeming feature of rarely sneering, but would sometimes beam in a hillbilly smile. His mother, my Mother's sister was from inbred stock that had moved to the city from the Pennines. He was a bit thick, some time before he had done three years in Pentonville Prison having been caught with a safe still in the boot of his car weeks after a robbery. He had been the wheels for a job and had been the fall Guy for the rest of the gang. Whether out of fear or misplaced loyalty he had taken the rap but did not grass on the others. Scarcely had we finished eating when Gordon rushed me off in a car more suited to carrying a dozen hoods, going from Dagenham to Barking in 12 minutes and then on into the City to see a film called the Blue Max about a first world air ace. This was Gordon's sixth time of seeing the film. The next day I went with him to a leafy suburb. A lady was paying Gordon to lay paving flags in her garden. He sprinkled a dusting of ashes over the grass and laid the slabs in a random fashion. The ladies husband was a Sea Captain and she probably thought it would be a nice surprise when he returned from the sea. I was standing, watching, my right foot bandaged. She brought him some tea, one cup for him none for me; southern hospitality. Gordon had his back to her and was re-living the film, he was shooting the Brits making a sound of machine guns and whine of aero engines, the woman stood, mouth open, too shocked to speak. Next day I went back north.

# 13

## EPILEPSY

I could not wear shoes until my toes had fully healed so for
now working on a building site was out of the question. Bob
Brigham employed me to do some joinery work in his climbing
shop. Another friend Brian Sullivan had got himself a job
in the Drawing office of a well known engineering firm,
Mather & Platts, as a trainee draughtsman. It seemed a step up
the tree for him, a mechanic, but he assured me it was easy to
get in. It was an eye opener. The hours were nine to five with an
hour off for dinner. There was a separate canteen for the office
workers, no dirty seats for them, and no clocking in and out. If
the men on the shop floor clocked in at 7:34 instead of 7:30 they
lost a quarter of an hour's pay. I was late most days but at the
end of each week the section boss would ask, ever so politely,
'Would you mind improving your time keeping?' The work
was basically unskilled, a rough drawing of a fire door and a list
of components needed, or an equally simple sketch of sprinkler
systems. Brian's drawings looked like a spider had dipped its
legs in ink and crawled across the drawing paper. After he left
Mather and Platts he started an agency for hiring draughtsmen
and became a millionaire. We spent some of our long dinner
time in the gym. The only way to get Brian involved with any
training was to play a game throwing a medicine ball at each
other hard enough to injure. Several times the ball collided
with my head. After one of these sessions I had an epileptic fit
the following morning, luckily at home. Apparently I had made
the scar tissue from my head injury two and a half years before,

bleed which caused the fit. That was Dr Tom Patey's theory. It was a huge shock. Weeks later after a session in the Grouse and a damp doss in a wet wood shed at Stoney Middleton I had another fit. One of the lads Keith Bancroft gave me a lift home to Barbara's flat. Keith and his wife could not have been more sympathetic. I was struck dumb and could not see beyond the immediate. The first fit could have been a one off, a second fit was not. Given my new medical status it would have made sense to have stayed at Mathers and not to tell them about the epilepsy, as an office worker a day off sick was paid. But the job was boring and leading nowhere so I left and went back to the building trade. I was sent to hospital for some tests and a consultation with a Neurologist. His words were 'No driving cars, no climbing ladders and definitely no climbing mountains' he never mentioned work. I had met Barbara my wife to be several weeks before this episode and I could have expected her to have scarpered. Less than a year later we were married.

The Alpine and Dolomite climbs I had done in the summers of 1964, '65 and '66 after recovering from a bad head injury had left an impression of fantastic rock faces often more in the sun than in the shadow. Facing up to the Doctors words about no climbing mountains or rocks would spell the end of such exploits. Some of the climbs such as the Phillip Flam the Andrich Fae or the Bonnatti pillar had at that time some status as major climbs for budding tigers. Most of the others were good quality hardish routes. Combined, they added up to thousands of feet of good climbing. I had had some fantastic times and many good memories. The onset of epilepsy made any lingering ambition to work as a climbing instructor out of the question. Only six months later I was offered a job at an outdoor centre in the Lake District, it was a permanent job instructing Manchester school children. I went to the interview to explain why I could not accept it. At the time I was working at a joinery workshop as a wood machinist, the neurologist never mentioned not to work with circular saws and other dangerous things. It was a sweat shop and to have started married life living and working in the Lake District would have been perfect.

# 14

## USEFUL OR USELESS

Sport is said to imbue youth with the necessary virtues to be hard working and trustworthy, which does not necessarily apply to climbing rocks. Mountaineering as opposed to purely rock climbing is different insomuch as it is more expensive so unless you are born rich, a person has to work hard to earn enough money to visit distant mountain ranges. Climbing Mountains, like working, can be masochistic. In the dismantling of the industrial parts of Britain the otherwise right wing government of Mrs Thatcher made it easy to sign on the dole, although not me I might add. Whereas this helped to produce a welfare dependant underclass, it was great for aspiring young crag rats. Like other dangerous sports, the adrenalin rush, the skill and the endorphins released from the exercise make the sport highly addictive and it can be done on the cheap. Climbing standards continued to rise and at even faster rate than hitherto. None of this could be described as useful by the toiling masses. To leave the freedom of the Gritstone edges, the wind the sun or the rain for a steady job becomes increasingly difficult as age turns youthful fecklessness into a lifestyle. This life style hardly encourages a strong work ethic and a consequent lack of skills needed to make a success of any opportunities that might come along. I belonged to an earlier generation so I served an apprenticeship first. After 5 years of day release, I took the final exam of the City & Guilds in Carpentry and Joinery, stayed half an hour, scrawled five questions, and then went off to the Roaches climbing. Predictably, I failed. At the time all that was needed to become a woodwork teacher in a secondary school with all the holidays that came along with the job was a City & Guilds and one 'O' Level in English. That would have been no problem, one of the lads with a degree in English used to take the exams for the others. He once got 90% for a lad who had failed the exam twice.

Fifty years later, now in our sixties and early seventies many are still clawing their way up climbing walls training for next year's anticipated break through. It is often hit or miss as to which kind of new hip you have had. Mine was the magic Birmingham Hip. Other climbers have got Carpal tunnel syndrome or Arthritic fingers and knees, many of us are active, many, like me, are also hypochondriacs surfing the net for the latest ailment. We are a drain on the NHS but on balance probably not that useless.

# 15

## MARRIED

I had got a fleeting glance of Barbara de Caux on the Biolay campsite in Chamonix in the summer of '65, her eyes averted, hiding behind her long red hair. Mick Burke was like a cat with two tails. He had chatted her up in Cassis near Marseille but she soon left and went off to Greece. Not exactly a hippy, just a girl in a short dress with a taste for adventure. Fifteen months later the sun had turned her hair a shade darker and her white skin cream and she had just got back from her travels. We met up at a club dinner. She asked for an orange juice, I came back from the bar with two; this was a cunning ruse, she expected the usual macho, 'look at how much I can drink' approach. Ten months later we got married. Forty years later we were leading through on a twelve pitch slab climb above the village of La Berarde in the Ecrin mountains in France. The climb was really good. On Stanage Edge in our youth we would fantasize about a mythical long clean slab just like this one. The day was hot and sunny. All around us were big jagged peaks. Accommodation in the Club Alpine Francais Refuge was perfect with good food and a room to our selves. The long red hair had turned a reddish brown, mine was white but if I had met a mystic in Robin Hood's cave who told me that fifty years later this would be my fate, I would have said yes how very nice now get real.

I moved into a flat with Barbara not long after meeting her. Doing what the Neurologist had told me to do, I had given up climbing. Instead we went walking. Often our walks would be along the top of a Gritstone edge or some exposed ridge in Wales. On one such Sunday I met by chance some climbers I knew on the lower tier of the Roaches. Tony Nichols 'Nick' had just powered his way up a greasy overhanging crack, called appropriately Crack of Gloom. Nobody wanted to do it so I borrowed some rock boots and seconded him. That was me back climbing. A few weeks later we got married in Southport registry office. Unable to contemplate going for a two week honeymoon without climbing I asked Nick to come with us. We arrived in Southport late for our own wedding in a wreck of a Mini Van. The registry man asked for another witness and I asked Nick to come forward. He had a black eye from a fight the week before and looked a bit of a bugger. My Mother and Father were already embarrassed by our flippant attitude to the wedding thing—although very pleased to have Barbara as a daughter in law, my Mother thought I was marrying above my station and it was not fair on the girl. Probably true.

# 16

## REGULAR WORK

Hopping from job to job having months off work supposedly to go climbing had run its course. Having no continuity in lifestyle had prevented me from keeping in touch with old friends or making proper new ones, I was never in one place long enough, and knowing dozens of people superficially is no substitute. We were living in an upstairs flat, just yards away from a bus stop and with a railway station minutes away. As young climbers our teenage assumptions about married life when discussed in Robin Hoods cave or wherever we were kipping assumed that there would be neither time nor money to be able to continue climbing. I could not have been more wrong. After a year working in a variety of sweatshops, I landed a job with a small plumbing firm in central Manchester, I was their only joiner. The boss never bothered me and the work was varied. Barbara had a job teaching art in an adult centre which she loved. For me to continue climbing and having the odd epileptic fit did not seem to bother her so that was fine. Life took on an immensely enjoyable routine. I began to do more solo climbing than hitherto in case I became short of climbing partners. Oddly enough I developed several climbing partners with Dave Little, Eddy Birch, Paul 'Tut' Braithwaite and occasionally Mike Kosterlitz and Adrian Liddel all prepared to climb with me, amazing really. Barbara had a driving licence and we bought an old van. We called him Snudge. She lined him with polystyrene tiles and under Tut's instructions gave him three coats of paint with a rub down between each coat

Tut was a time served painter and decorator and the excessive paint job he advised Barbara to do was just a wind up. The van broke irreparably a few month later. Our next car was a Nash Metropolitan—a car made for American housewives. It had a large front seat an inaccessible boot and a column change of three gears and was totally impractical. The garage man, who sold it to us, had Barbara regrind the valves, no mean feet and very labour intensive, after which the car lasted us three years including two trips to the Alps. We called the car George. For the next three winters we climbed mostly on Craig Gogarth in North Wales or Derbyshire limestone and in summer the higher crags of Wales and the Lake District and one evening a week after work on Grit. These next four years were very productive some days stand out more than others...

# 17

## THE VIKING WEEKEND

That weekend Barbara had something on so instead of taking our van, five of us squeezed into Tut's Ford Anglia. Brackenclose is an FRCC climbing club hut situated in the remotest of the Lake District valleys, Wasdale. At the time the hut was fairly basic, but it is sighted at the start of the path to Scafell making it very convenient. The place is steeped in history — the nearby Crags on Great Gable and Scafell are the birth place of English rock Climbing. The next morning a June sun was streaming through the windows. When Dave, Eddy and I arrived at Mickledore the sun was fully on the East Buttress the rock dry and light gray, Tut was behind with his girlfriend Julie, climbing solo I could maybe get a climb done before he arrived. Mickledore Grooves, a 3 star VS, was the perfect start, warm firm rock, not too difficult, the climbing is varied and never insecure, a good start to a perfect day. When Tut arrived our first climb was a route called Leverage first ascended by Robin Smith in 1958. The climb is now graded HVS, the first pitch is 5b the second pitch is 5a. In the early years of the Alpha club we would only tick a climb in the guidebook if we had led the crux. Sometimes I would untie and solo the crux pitch to get another tick, I suppose this was annoying but I did not stop to think. This is how we did Leverage. We then climbed Phoenix, put up in 1957 by Ron Moseley, a contemporary of Joe Brown and Don Whillans. Hugh Banner, who knew Moseley, said that when at his best Moseley equalled them in ability, although his form was very erratic. At the time of its first ascent, although not realised then, it was the hardest climb on the crag. The climb is now graded E1 with two pitches of 5b. Our next climb was Hell's Groove, a famous climb, first climbed by Pete Greenwood and Arthur Dolphin in 1952. These two men were rivals for the number one slot of 'best climber' in the Lake District at the time of this ascent. They seldom teamed up together, but if they had who knows what they could have achieved. Dolphin was killed in the Alps not long after and Greenwood stopped climbing to become a business man. His reputation as a climber has been forgotten and the only time I watched him climb was one wet Sunday afternoon in 1963. We left the pub and went bouldering in Rosthwaite quarry, Greenwood had not climbed in years and was in leather shoes, a suit and was half drunk. He still managed to climb some thin problems on a slate slab. After Hell's Groove we went out of the sun and in to the shadow to climb Trinity HVS 5a-5a-4c we both climbed solo, then dropped a grade to solo Morning Wall MVS together. Tut went off to find Julie. In little less than a month we would be in the Alps. Mountaineering needs total trust in your companion; not to fall when moving together and to have an easy accord with rope work. Some empathy and humour helps to make the experience even better. Tut was already very fit so the fitter I was the better for us both so I carried on climbing. Dave and Eddy were waiting for me on Mickledore it would be nice to walk down together. For my seventh route of the day I chose Overhanging Wall: HVS 5a, 4b, put up in 1933 by Maurice Linnell and A. T. Hargreaves. In the opinion of Steve Dean in his book *Hands of a Climber*, Maurice Linnell was quite simply one of the undisputed geniuses of British rock climbing. A. T. Hargreaves was another great climber of that generation. The first pitch was a bit scary some sideways moves often brought the floor into view. The rest of the climb is up a slab and I quickly forgot my growing nervousness. The descent down Broad Stand was getting repetitive but I had another climb in me before Dave and Eddy got sick of waiting. Chartreuse: 54 m

E1 5a–5a was another Robin Smith route, his untimely death in the Pamirs was a great loss to British and Scots climbing not least because of his quirky character. He was only 23 and was already one of the best mountaineers of his generation... This was my eighth climb of the day and the second E1. I felt good and in some ways found it easier than Overhanging Wall as it was not yet in the shadow. In North Wales I had soloed harder climbs but for the sheer quantity and quality only one other day, a year before, on Clogwyn Du'r Arddu in North Wales had been as good. Three of the routes had first been climbed in 1931, 1932 and 1933. The other five climbs between 1952 and 1958. The sheer lack of protection these climbers had available to them, either pumps or nailed boots on their feet, hemp rope, line hemp slings and steel karabiners, often hardly strong enough to hold body weight let alone a fall is often forgotten. These guys seldom used pitons. In fact they might as well have soloed those first ascents for all the security they had. Back down at Brackenclose instead of cooking I mixed a bowl of chocolate mousse and sat on the steps watching the sun set, strangely I was neither tired nor reflective but was just wishing the others would hurry up before the pub shut. The weather on Sunday morning was just as good.

Years before Alan Atkinson had fallen off a nasty overhanging crack on the Tophet Wall of Great Gable. Les Brown had spied the line and had sent Ackers up the crack to try and arrange some runners before Les himself had a go. Dangling his weight off a loose spike Ackers broke his ankle when the spike came off. Me and Tut thought that as we were climbing well we would go and have a look. A film doing the rounds at the time when Ackers had his accident was called the Vikings. The lads fancied themselves as latter day Vikings as they shot around on big motorbikes shouting Odin, so it seemed appropriate to call the climb the Vikings in memory of that era; that is if we could get up it. The crack was very overhanging and did not look to have any resting places. Yesterdays soloing exploits were potentially dangerous but within my limits, today's scheme might well exceed them. Tut led the first pitch. As I started up the crack on the second pitch a voice of reason was urging me to go down but against my better judgement I pressed on. I knew I was not strong enough to place many runners even if there were any to place, although a placement for a Moac appeared low down, it was to be my last runner. A sequence of moves not far above the runner consisted of using a pinch grip then moving rapidly up and thrusting my left hand into a jam before my right hand slid off the pinch. Only momentum stopped me coming off. In the future such a tenuous manoeuvre would become a normal technique, it helped when equipment improved but at the time it felt very dodgy. On the next sequence of moves I was getting too knackered to stop and think and anyway this would only have stopped the seamless flow of arms and legs which was disconnected from my brain. Above the crack was a kind of niche, my feet were on a small ledge but the bulging side walls were pushing me off. There was a crack in the back of the niche but it was too far in to reach. I could stand there and although nearly sliding out I was no longer hanging on my arms and could for the moment take in my situation, the moac was not far above Tut, which meant a fall on these next moves could be terminal. Moving up and out of the niche felt very insecure. Above I arrived on a decent ledge, but my throat was dry and feeling a nervous wreck I looked in vain for a belay and worried about the way ahead. Eventually I settled down and the solutions to both problems were obvious. The Vikings was for a short time the hardest climb in the Lake District. A comment in a magazine of the period by Pete Livesey speaks about the climb, '*The Vikings (Gable) climbed by McHardy—a ferocious Whillansian type ascent and harder than anything else in the Lakes.*' Coming from one of the leading lights of the near future this was praise indeed.

# LAKELAND COMMENTARY

Richard McHardy's fierce route, The Vikings (opposite), typifies the high level of fitness and boldness needed to tackle top-standard Lakeland climbs in the 'seventies. Here, Pete Livesey, one of the leading activists, casts a critical eye over the decades of past development and the current period of urgency ethical debate.

**The Vikings** (Gable) climbed by McHardy — a ferocious Whillansian type ascent and harder than anything else in the Lakes.

ON FORK LIGHTNING CRACK, HEPTONSTALL QUARRY

PHOTOGRAPH BY: GENEROUS GUY FORGOTTEN HIS NAME

## 18

## LLECH DDU

The Great Arête put up by Ed Drummond was special, not necessarily because of its technical standard but its improbable line. 'Is your name McHardy?' Me and Dave Little were stood on a sea washed ledge, we had abseiled down overhanging grass and pulled the ropes down after us. If we could not do our proposed climb then we were stuck. The man asking the question told us his name, Ed Ward—Drummond. 'You did the second ascent of my route, The Strand last week. Did you find it exceptionally hard?' 'No' I lied, 'I find every hard route hard.' I could have added that we did find the climb hard and very good but his overweening confidence was so at odds with the nervous state I was in as I looked up at Wendigo that I did not feel like being truthful.

Two years later me and Tut were walking in to Llech Ddu, a large dark unstable crag in the Carneddau. For a few years the cliff enjoyed a lot of attention on account of two climbs in particular, The Great Corner and The Big Groove. They were good lines and when I had climbed them they were fairly clean and sound. Dominating the middle of the crag is an overhanging arête. On the nose of the arête is a narrow groove. One side of the groove is just off vertical, the other side is overhanging. The groove as a whole is set at the same wildly overhanging angle as the Main Arête. The climb was another of Ed Ward—Drummond's creations and waited a second ascent. We thought that it looked impossible. Rumours abounded that Drummond used novel ways to place protection, such as taking his weight on a bat hook and other devious tricks. Looking up at this horrendous line made us wish we had not been so full of hubris. The first move into the groove would be difficult to reverse and a fall from the groove held by an imaginary good runner would have the climber dangling in space above the first pitch with insufficient rope to be lowered off. This was before harnesses, belay plates and 50 m ropes were used. What protection I eventually managed to place was half way up the groove and not good, it seemed unlikely that Drummond would have fared much better, bat hooks or not. The climbing was hard scary and strenuous, the right wall of the groove just keeps trying to push your body out in to space. After the groove ended the way ahead went through several overhangs, before this there was a place to rest and a piton, left there from the first ascent. This was my first good runner. When solo climbing you try and leave a bit in reserve, normally when roped up you can often contrive to escape, but now even if I fully trusted this piton I did not have enough rope to abseil off. Using a short crack for my right hand to lay away on, with my feet up high I made a tentative reach above the first bulge. Nothing immediately came to hand and a fall might rip the piton. Using the piton for my right hand offered more security and if I had to reverse, it would make the manoeuvre possible. Above was another bulge I found one more piton in a horizontal crack beneath the final overhang. This peg was really sound and I did not need to use it for aid but only to clutch hold of, scared witless. Above the overhang I was hoping for some kind of ledge to belay on, but instead had to accept a large foot hold and just a couple of dodgy flakes to tie onto. Having Tut on the other end of the rope made the position half tenable, the trust and communication between us was telepathic. When his face appeared he seemed stuck for words, I said 'That was psychedelic' he stuttered 'That was the word I was thinking of.' Our ascent had used one pull on a peg, more for safety than technical need. Tut led through, this last pitch was not hard but loose with only token protection. He had given his then girlfriend the keys to his car; she was booked on a course starting that night at Plas-y-Brenin which was miles away. Our route back took us over Carnedd Llewelyn and Carnedd Dafydd and down into the Ogwen valley, leaving us several miles walk along the road to Capel Curig. The walk back turned a good day into a memorable one. The beauty of the hills and the freedom of movement after being virtually crag fast was really pleasant and mellow. An enquiry as to whether we could have the car keys elicited a reply for us to wait until after a lecture so she could get a lift to the pub. We were starving hungry, tired and nervously knackered, waiting on a form outside the Brenin. It had been five years earlier that I had left my job as a maintenance man, went to the Alps and never returned, except to claim back wages; it felt strange. Given the gear climbers like Drummond had or did not have, The Great Arête, in my opinion, was very impressive. The first free ascent was five years later in 1975 by Pete Livesey and Steve Foster and the climb is now graded E4 6a. The practice of writing up first free ascents that became normal by the late seventies could only be accurate if it was possible to know for certain that nobody else had done that route free. This also applies to second ascents and the practice relied to a large degree for information in CC or FRCC hut books. In part there was also sometimes an implied idea that the first ascent of a climb used unnecessary aid. By the mid seventies manufactured gear included Hexentrics, small aluminium wedges on wire and Chouinard stoppers—this was a far cry from placing pitons, chock stones or nuts in overhanging rock when the next runner was hypothetical. There was also the difficulty of climbing past an aid point on poor holds, so once aid was used it could lead to more aid being used than appeared necessary. With decent runners it is often the case that climbing a move free is easier than swinging about on gear. This comment is not as opinionated or critical as it may seem, just an observation that many first ascents that used some aid were nonetheless amazingly bold.

# 19

## PINNACLE GIRDLE AND WOUBITS LEFT HAND

In the late sixties we were allowed to drive cars along way up farm tracks towards Clogwyn Du'r Arddu but it involved lots of hill starts to open and shut the many gates. Without a hand brake or the right amount of finesse this treatment was forced to bugger up the gears. After that particular Friday night Snudge died but it did give us an early start. Our objective was the Girdle Traverse of the pinnacle E3 5c. 590 feet. Described in the 1989 guide book as one of the finest routes in Wales. The pinnacle is above the East Buttress so to save a scramble we soloed Chimney route 360 ft VS. The rock was dry, but at eight in the morning still cold. Between the two tiers of crags is some high angled grass called by the Oldies the Green Gallery, above which is the stunning pinnacle. From the first few feet the climb is very exposed and remains so for its length, always open, never surrounded by the sides of a groove or an overhanging crack. It really feels like floating in the sky. With the limited protection then available and the sustained nature of the climbing this route could only be described as a Tour de force. After a frightening overhanging abseil the girdle finishes up a climb called Shrike, a steep wall with some good holds and still in the late morning sun. Leo Dickenson appeared looking down the shrike wall with a large camera. Leo went on to be a world class adventure cameraman doing all sorts of crazy stunts. It felt good on the top, our days climbing finished, then Leo had the idea of me and Tut doing another route whilst he took some more photographs. We agreed and went with him

BELAYING TUT BRAITHWAITE BEGINNING THE HAND TRAVERSE ON OUR ASCENT OF
THE PINNACLE GIRDLE—PHOTOGRAPH BY: LEO DICKINSON

CLIMBING SECOND PITCH OF WOUBITS LEFT HAND, BELAYING BY TUT BRAITHWAITE

PHOTOGRAPH BY: LEO DICKINSON

TUT BRAITHWAITE LEADING THE TOP PITCH OF WOUBITS LEFT HAND

PHOTOGRAPH BY: LEO DICKINSON

to the Far East Buttress, he would abseil into position and we would climb Woubits Left Hand, first climbed in 1959 by Joe Brown and a seventeen-year old Martin Boysen. After two 5b pitches the third used some precarious aid. Leo got his pictures and we had a fantastic day. In 1968 it was considered a hard day. Rock climbing can consist of a series of physically difficult moves where strength and technique are paramount or it can be a scary ballet in an exposed and unprotected environment, the Pinnacle Girdle is a good example of the latter.

# 20

## AN ACCIDENT AT WORK

The Drugs for epilepsy almost worked. I only had on average three fits a year, although they were grand mal. With hindsight the reason for them was usually associated with either a high temperature or a lack of blood sugar. Alcohol can play a part in either. It took me years to work this out. One Monday morning found me doing dry rot repairs to a huge roof beam. The tower scaffold was not high enough so I was balanced on a pile of bricks. We had been to a club dinner on the Saturday and I still had a hangover. When the bricks collapsed I plummeted, head first, glancing a big old radiator with my head and shoulder. I then had a fit, or was it the other way round? After what seemed an age stuck on a trolley in a draughty hospital corridor Barbara appeared to take me home. In the next month the hurt shoulder was a nuisance on a couple of occasions. Tut got an invite from some cavers to go with them down a cave, by way of a treat and for support he took me and Woody. Somewhere in the Yorkshire Dales we parked by the road and surveyed the rain, the three cavers donned wet suits over a dozen thermals. All we had were two pairs of jeans and two pullovers. Tut was fascinated, watching them dress. Me and Woody set off up the hill, we stopped to look at a neat little feature shaped like a horse trough, water appeared from the ground and disappeared again after about five feet, it was no more than 24 inches wide and about the same deep. Chief caver appeared, knelt down in the trough plunged his head under water and squirmed out of sight. We followed suit but my damaged shoulder made crawling on

BELAYED BY EDDY BIRCH. BAMFORD EDGE—DERBYSHIRE

TUT WITH HAIR, CLOGGY – LATE 60'S

hands and knees difficult, gasping for air I was both pleased and amazed to exit into a large passage. Tut started to show off and using his spidery physique was bridging across either wall whilst we waded through chest deep cold water. A hole appeared where the water plunged sixty feet into a subterranean river. Chief tied us all onto a rope and we climbed across the void after which came some ladder pitches. What little water was running in this new passage, Tut kept on sitting in to form a damn then would stand up letting it cascade on to one particular guy's head, God knows why he felt such animosity, perhaps it was the man who had given him the invite. Chief decided we should retreat. He belayed me and Woody over the hole first and told us to make our way out. We got lost. I was trying to get my head through a hole when Dave suggested that where we had been before was not that small. We had gone up the wrong passage. My bad shoulder prevented a fast crawl or even a doggy paddle in my attempt to keep up with Dave. If we did not meet up with the others we were stuffed. But we did. Once outside there was a cold wind and my teeth were going like castanets, Tut gave me a sly kick and said 'Stop shivering they'll think we're soft ★★★★★.' The cafe in Ingleton sold whopping big cakes.

# 21

## WOUBITS

The Welsh three-thousanders make an amazingly good hill walk although it is technically a walk rather than a climb / scramble. As an experience it is almost on a par with the Cuillin ridge. We set off in the dark accompanied by Dave Alcock, he knew the way. We could not read a map so we could hardly have disagreed with Dave's navigation as we stumbled over the Carneddau but we did finish up in Ogwen. Dave hitch hiked home for his breakfast. On our way up Tryfan we climbed the Long chimney climb on terrace wall and the first part of Snowdon by way of a gully above Nant Peris. In the gully we found a black cable which we used on the steep bits pulling hand over hand up the grot until we came to a big dish, it was the television aerial for the village. Descending Snowdon down Cwm Glas, the evening sun was turning the scree red except where the north facing crags were casting shadows. At the hut, with amazing timing, Barbara had just cooked the tea. Paul Nunn had appeared, gone to the pub and said he would see us later. He was on his own and so tomorrow we would have to climb as a three. Whoever won the toss to lead could not be allowed to steal a plumb, so we chose a route that had nothing to commend it. In the event I won the toss and led the direct start to East Gully Groove. Tut and myself had previously done Woubits Left Hand but I had a fancy to climb the regular Woubits. I left Paul and Tut and went over to the Far East Buttress. Scrambling down the Far Eastern Terrace to the start of the climb is a forbidding place at the best of times but now it was deserted, silent except for the menacing croak of a raven. The first pitch is a bold 5b but I had climbed it before and that gave me some confidence. I was dragging a rope in case I needed to try and escape but it only increased my weight. The next pitch although very steep had grass growing in the most unlikely places, the first ascent had been made fifteen years earlier in 1955 and it was obvious by the amount of grass and grot that in the intervening years the climb had not become a trade route. Half way up the pitch I thought I had bitten off more than I could chew, keeping cool on difficult but sound rock is one thing but the way ahead looked anything but sound. A fall if not immediately fatal would entail a long wait before being found so anything that offered even a vestige of hope was worth trying. I tied a large loop in the rope and clipped into a runner which I left behind. The idea that this might hold was an illusion but it settled my nerves. On the top of the climb I met two of the Cambridge university club, we were chatting away as I pulled in the rope, when the end appeared they looked shocked 'Where's Tut?' One of them asked, 'I don't know, he never could tie a bowline,' I replied.

Paul and Tut had gone to do a climb called the Boldest. I needed company so I went to find them. At the bottom of the route were gathered a bunch of the lads. It was one of those magical moments when things come together. Tut and Paul were over the crux and Alan Rouse was soloing the route behind them. Sat around on the grass were Leo Dickenson, Pete Minks, Cliff Phillips, Eric Jones and Brian Molyenue. The best bunch of solo climbers about at the time. Eric had soloed the Bonatti pillar on the Dru and a few years later soloed the North face of the Eiger. Among the notable ascents Peter Minks made was a solo ascent of the Walker Spur on the Grande Jorrasse. Cliff Phillips achieved a lot of impressive solo ascents and Leo went on to have all sorts of amazing adventures as an extreme sports cameraman, usually with Eric. They were all watching and willing Alan on, enjoying each others company, no matter what happened in the rest of our lives the camaraderie of that Sunday afternoon must bring back happy memories to us all. Moss Groove is a climb that starts half way up the crag and acts as an alternative finish to Great Slab. Pete Minks curled a finger at me, it was time to go and solo something else. As we traversed into the groove, a shadow past on our left. It was Cliff dressed in black going fast but silently up Great Slab, somewhere behind was Leo, out of breath, not a hope in hell of keeping up with Cliff, but trying his hardest.

ALAN ROUSE – TREMADOC, 1960S

PHOTOGRAPH BY: LEO DICKINSON

# 22

## CENOTAPH CORNER

'Looking at you is making me feel nervous.' Great, just what I needed, some bloke safely belaying his mate telling me that I was making him feel nervous. Cenotaph Corner forms the most impressive rock feature in Llanberis Pass, shaped like a huge 120 ft open book with vertical smooth side walls. The pocket filled rock make some of the climbs easier than they look but even so the least difficult of the climbs is given the name Cemetery Gates, which was where the speaker was belayed, on a foot wide ledge about 40 ft away. One hundred and ten feet of cenotaph was beneath me and a further hundred foot of easier angled rock below this. I only had about ten foot of difficult climbing left. His words made me aware of what I looked like from his perspective which was terrifying. With no rope I was bridged across the corner in a feature called the niche, one of the few places where you could take some weight off your arms and with the security of a piton in my hand I was feeling half safe. This was still before climbing harnesses but I had a tape sling knotted around my waist and I was carrying a couple of slings round my neck, if I clipped the three of these together and into the piton it might offer some protection whilst I climbed out of the niche before unclipping the slings. Above and safely on the big, tree filled ledge, my pleasure and relief were only tempered by the thought of the slings I had left behind clipped to the piton. The other two climbers were now on the ledge and offered me the use of their rope to abseil down the corner so that I could retrieve the slings. Using a good tree as the main belay I walked back across the ledge and passed the ropes around the back of a sapling so that they hung down the corner and not down the right wall. I never asked them what the length of their rope was and with only a sit sling and no abseil device I set off down the corner. Having rescued my slings, concentration disappeared and I was making little jumps going too fast and behaving like I was already in the pub. I heard Barbara with her mate Julie at the bottom of the crag and looked down. Ten foot below was the end of the rope, with another thirty foot to go before the bottom of the corner and another hundred before the floor, I was in deep shit. There used to be some quarter weight nylon slings jammed in a thread which made an in situ runner, so I clipped into this with my sit sling and after a lot of shouting instructions got the two lads to flick the ropes from behind the sapling to give me some extra rope. The rope then went in a steep angle up the right wall. It was hopeless trying to take in much rope but the minute I took my weight off the threaded sling I would drop with the stretch of the rope and pendulum across the wall. Would the rope be long enough? It was almost but I had to leave go for the last two foot and grab a tree!

A year later I was taking a German climber up Cenotaph, he was on an exchange visit with the Climbers Club. The last ten foot above the niche was wet and I began to reverse back into the niche to sort out my runners for a final sortie. Pulling upwards on the peg it came sliding slowly out and I fell. After about seventy foot Albert held me. He was wearing a kind of makeshift chest harness using a slip knot, which when in the future it got known in Britain was called an Italian hitch. Never having seen anything like it, I was amazed when he stopped me falling. The piton could hardly have been the original but old nonetheless, and it was the one I had pulled on the year before. I went back up and hammered an angle peg in up to the hilt. If the piton had popped out the year before, I would have landed by Barbara and Julie's feet.

# 23

## VECTOR

I first climbed Vector in the summer of '63. There were four pitons in situ for runners and two for the belay after the first pitch. The ochre coloured slab on the first pitch is now the crux, back then it was not polished and the crux was near the top of the climb. Vector had a reputation for being technically difficult, but the first time I climbed it every move fell into place and I did not find the climb too desperate. In 1969 Vector reputedly had not had a solo ascent, feeling on form I convinced myself that I could. Climbing and exiting from the ochre slab I remembered exactly the moves I had made six years before and was feeling good. After passing the belay ledge the climb traverses to the left before ascending the head wall which looked frightening but by now it was too late for backing down. The tree canopy was a lot smaller than it is today and on the traverse left it was impossible not to look at the floor 100 ft below. I remembered the final moves being strenuous and insecure, so on the moves up to them I was taking great care to have my feet high enough to avoid having to use the first thing I could reach. This was where everything was in the balance; while I had been placing and replacing my feet my arms had got tired and I still had the final strenuous moves to go. With great relief my fingers found reasonably good holds, the finger cracks that had been shallow, were now cleaner and deeper. Very chuffed, I pulled out on to easy ground. The place was quiet and then shouts of relief and congratulations came up from the road as the different groups started motorbikes and vehicles up and headed home. Impressed or unimpressed was beside the point, the heartening emotion was that they were pleased to see that one of the tribe would not be missing from the pub the next weekend. The climb is now graded E3 5c but the rock as become so polished that the climb is no longer the gem it once was. Over the last forty five years the trees have grown considerably, the road as been rebuilt slightly nearer the crag and there is a lot more traffic on the roads, all of which as changed the ambiance of that part of Tremadoc. This is all the more apparent to somebody who has only had a few visits back to a place they once knew and loved.

# 24

## THE GROOVES

In 1970 we were climbing The Skull a 420 ft E4, 6a climb on Cyrn Las, a magnificent crag in Llanberis Pass. I was with a friend of ours Lyn Noble. Behind us in a rope of three came Tut, Dave Little and Ed Birch. After doing one climb Lyn had to go back to the Lakes so instead of hanging about I set off to solo The Grooves hoping to finish before the lads had topped out on The Skull. I had done the climb before in 1962 with Les Brown but he had led the second pitch which had contained the then crux, in the event the crack was clean and it was now no harder than the rest of the climb. A variation for the third pitch is called the Overhanging Arête, its grade is now E2 5b. At the time the pitch was not considered very hard, however the position and commitment gave it a reputation. Without a rope this would be greatly magnified. The first part of this final pitch starts on the left wall of a groove followed by a traverse out left to some big spikes on a ridiculously exposed arête. A good grass ledge under this pitch offers some respite but it only served for me to sit and ponder what hare brained whim had got me there. With harder solo ascents behind me and with the first two pitches already done it should be OK. Once at the spikes both my hands and nerves were tired, The Skull had been hard and strenuous, I had also been rushing too much. It is possible to get a forearm around the first spike and have a rest. The steepness prohibits staying there long and fear progressively saps any bottle. I had some tape tied around my waist so I threaded a quarter weight sling through an old rusty peg and clipped it to the tape then climbed above the flakes. I could find no holds good enough for any upward progress so I climbed back down to the spikes. It seemed improbable that I would have the strength for a successful second try. The piton had been inserted by Banner in 1958 and any chance of it holding a fall was nil. Convinced I was as good as dead it became apparent that whilst I was tied into the sling like a kind of umbilical cord I would not have the freedom to reach any further than before, so I unclipped. At first I still couldn't reach anything good enough, a move left entailed looking down at where I could place a foot, Cwm Glass was everywhere below. Out left a handhold did appear and with 360 ft below my feet I made the final moves onto easy ground. On the top of the crag the boys were still coiling ropes. I had planned to jump out of nowhere to scare them, instead I could only whisper a nervous hello.

# 25

## MOTIVATION

The weather was unusually hot, tramps and old prostitutes were lying about in Back Piccadilly swigging cheap Australian white wine. In a back alley between Market Street and Canon Street I watched a tramp discover a pot of yoghurt in a rubbish skip. He carefully placed it on the edge of the skip, slowly rolled up his sleeves, pulled out a spoon and with great delight ate the yoghurt. A millionaire eating a bucket of caviar could not have been as pleased. I could hardly have looked much better than the tramps. I was working as a jobbing joiner in the very centre of Manchester walking from one small job to another with a bass of tools and carpet slippers on my feet complete with holes in the toes but more comfortable than shoes. I arrived at one spot to do a temporary mend on a door which had been damaged in a burglary. The owner went ballistic shouting for me to get out and not giving me the chance to explain that I was the joiner come to mend the door. On the Wednesday evening after work I was out on Stanage still in my slippers. I ran into a geek we knew who worked for the tax, and suddenly the city with all its class divisions and divisive values was perched back on my shoulders. He asked, 'Why were you and Tut spending all last Saturday on West Buttress Eliminate?' We had not spent that long in fact, but that was not the point. Pissed off I told him to fuck off or follow me... Then I set off soloing Right Unconquerable. Near the top are a series of horizontal rounded cracks utterly useless in my slippers. Such an act of petulance should have spelt disaster but on reflection I could understand what motivated me. For many climbers and hill walkers the expression 'The freedom of the hills' really did mean that. Back at work in the city many of us had jobs with a lack of status that others could deride but once among the crags a different hierarchy pertained and if you were lucky none at all. This freedom from being stifled by other people's restrictive values is what motivated us into hanging about under some dripping overhang watching the rain as we bullshitted about some previous epic.

# 26

Tut went to the Alps with the Burnley lads in Dave Barton's Land Rover, I should have gone with them as the company must have been great. The first thing they did was to race each other unroped up the Hornli ridge on the Matterhorn. In Chamonix the weather was bad. Mo & Jackie had left a candle burning in their tent and when they returned the tent had burned to the floor so they went home. Eddy Birch and myself did a route in a storm. Sick of crawling around a wet tent cooking, me and Barbara made a shed, some German lads gave me some nails and we found an old tent by the river which made the roof. With only a week of our holidays left the weather turned fine and Tut appeared. We decided to climb the Gervasutti Pillar on Mont Blanc du Tacul, it is 800 m long graded TD with a lot of pitches of 5sup and one or two easy grade 6. The route finishes near the summit at a height of 4,248 m. After weeks of doing nothing, altitude might be a problem, at least for me. We met about seven o'clock by the Midi téléphérique, Tut was eating a hard boiled egg which probably left him with an energy deficit but not cooking gave him an extra half hour in bed. After descending from the Aiguille du Midi into the glacier basin of the Valley Blanche, a huge orange pillar facing south and in the sun all day soared up to a blue sky from the white of the snow surrounding it. The climbing was sustained but never desperate, most of the stances were good and afforded some rest. The last few pitches climbed up a lovely sharp arête but the sun had departed and it was good to arrive at the summit. The view was amazing. We were looking down on a storm thousands of feet beneath us, thunder and lightning just hundreds of feet above the valley. Around us and all over the summit of Mont Blanc the snow had turned mauve as the light from the setting sun brushed through the cloud. Before global warming took its toll the descent to the Col Midi was easy and before it was completely dark we reached the Refuge. The hut warden was in a corner talking to a small group of people. We thought we had a tin of corned beef and a packet of dried potatoes, the warden took it off us to prepare. As it was cooking the warden whispered to the group as if he was telling a smutty joke. I kicked Tut's shins under the table and muttered for him to eat whatever we got without changing his expression. The plates arrived, surrounding the corn beef was some yellow stuff. Barbara had bought us powdered maze by mistake. She met us the next morning and we took her down the Geant ice fall and the Mer du Glace for a treat. Crampons off crampons on, by the time she got to Montenvers she was knackered. We left her riding down on the train and set off in a hurry down the path and took what we thought was a short cut, but we were soon lost. A blaze mark on a tree indicated the makings of a new path, it was hellish steep but the trees marked for demolition continued vertically down the hill. By the time we realised that the marks must have been a boulder rolling downhill we were not far above the valley and so we continued on a vertical line. We came out of the trees and into a kind of field with the glacier river about 100 yards away, some caravans and tents were there, it was a club from Marseille and they seemed to have the place to themselves. We made the mistake of telling people and it became the new Biolay. Snell's field, as it was called, continued in use for years. With only days to go it would be a shame to waste our acclimatisation so we headed for the Sentinal Rouge on the Brenva face of Mont Blanc. Big Bob came with us. At the Trident bivi hut were four French lads, they were all rugby players and so was Bob. Normally at that time mixing French and English climbers was like mixing oil and water. These four were great. On the climb we moved together almost all the way, conditions were perfect, the French team were going slightly faster but Bob and themselves kept shouting the names of famous rugby players, competing to see how many they all knew. On the summit they had made a brew for us. Big Bob Ainley was a really good bloke and happily married to Nancy. He was killed descending the Hornli ridge of the Matterhorn in winter, with his friend Pete Brooke.

The summer of '69 Tut came to the Alps with us in our car. 'George' only had one long bench seat and somewhere in France the exhaust fell off, so we tied it up with some wire and a sling and got it fixed at home, six weeks later. Before the motorways were made travelling through rural France had a quiet charm and you could kip anywhere. Away from the motorways it still has but we are now too old to sleep anywhere but in a bed. Snell's field was already occupied by other Brits, I felt like telling them to bugger off, that me and Tut found the place the year before. On balance the Biolay campsite was better, it was near the shops and bars, had trees in isolated clumps, good for shade and the ground not being at the side of a glacier stream was better for placing tent pegs. For people who appreciated toilet facilities and warm water for washing the Biolay had reached the limits of hygiene and in any case it was being redeveloped. Snell's field at least had a glacier stream for washing your hands.

The year before we had noticed a large wide couloir to the right of the Gervasutti pillar, it looked straight forward and going all the way to the top of Mont Blanc du Tacul would be good for acclimatizing. We climbed the first third in the evening by an avalanche runnel, then sat for a few hours until in the early hours of the morning head torches appeared. We waited for the four French climbers to pass and then ascended easily the rest of the couloirs in their deep steps.

The North face of the Triolet is near the top of the Argentière glacier. Grade TD- 750 m, it was at the time a famous ice climb but in the years since has shrunk and has become dangerous. We roughly followed our previous plan by getting started in the evening, walked past the Argentière hut and sat on our sacks under the climb until midnight. Walking up the glacier in the afternoon sun had given us wet feet, I had forgotten my gloves but Barbara had stuffed spare socks in my sack so we climbed with one glove and one wet sock each on our hands. We were cold, hungry and apprehensive. Looked at head on, the face looked improbably steep but I discovered that with your back to the face, looked at upside down beneath your legs made the angle of the face appear less steep. Head torches appeared way down by the hut, it was a relief to be moving but an even bigger relief when we found the crux section had steps chopped and even an ice peg of the old drive in cut out kind in situ. Above we climbed together and were on the summit by the first light of dawn. We sat and waited whilst the two parties behind us started the descent. Our idea was to let them find any crevasses, which duly happened. Having helped extract the man we hoped they would invite us for a drink in the Couvercle hut but when no such offer was made we continued our descent. It was probably one of those cultural differences, they probably thought an official invite was not needed, or they might have been just miserable sods. Tut had a desire to climb the North face of the Eiger. The thought filled me with dread, the souls of dozens of dead climbers strewn up the face and the sheer size of the effort put me off the idea. It could wait for next year.

The Croz Spur on the Grande Jorasses still awaited a British ascent. Being next to the more famous Walker Spur, not much was known about the climb. This gave me the daft idea that it could possibly be a hidden gem. At the Refuge Leschaux we met two Kiwis, Graham Dingle and Murray

Jones. The Grande Jorrasses was the last of the six great north faces on their itinerary. One of them had already climbed the Walker Spur but an ascent of the Croz would give them the tick without repeating the Walker. With little persuasion they joined up with us. The first section was by way of a fairly steep snow slope of perfect névé. Graham and his friend Murray were very experienced on this kind of terrain and tackled it with great speed and competence. Pride and not wishing to be behind them on the rest of the climb spurred us on to a pace faster than normal so that we arrived at the first rocks just in front of them. Seconding the first pitch I dislodged a block which caused Murray to jump onto the narrow ledge where Graham, minus belay, was paying out their rope. By some miracle Murray maintained his balance avoiding almost certain death for them both. Apart from some verglas, this part of the climb was OK except that there were very little in situ pitons, (as was the case for the whole route) which made route finding difficult. After this came an ice field, three or four hundred feet of rock hard ice. Front pointing was out of the question; once started it would have been impossible to stop and place protection. Unless we climbed the ice field without any security or a rest the only option was to chop steps all the way. I went first and for all the hard work each step was scarcely bigger than a nick. It was very dodgy. We had joined forces but given my lack of step cutting experience we had the wrong man in front. A fall by any of the four of us would have had to be held by the occasional ice peg. At last I made the next rock section and could fix a belay. Above us was an ice chocked vertical groove and the appearance of a piton suggested that this had once been the way but was now all but impossible. After a traverse left for a pitch we found a vertical groove. It looked difficult and unclimbed so I set off with every available rock piton expecting the worst. After two reasonable pitches we came to another snow field which after a few hundred feet became triangular and led into a short chimney. Graham and Tut had a difference of opinion as to whether to continue up the chimney or traverse right to the foot of a big corner. On the traverse across the ice Tut gently touched rock that appeared to be part of the mountain. It was a block shaped like an enormous doughnut which slid off heading for Murray. He was belayed in a corner between ice and rock a hundred foot below. It could so easily have squashed him, only his crash hat made contact and that was cut so badly as to make it useless. At the bottom of the corner was a slab which by its broken appearance had not been exposed from under the ice for long. There were no belays and the first part of the corner was decomposed granite, as loose as it gets, and although becoming sounder, became difficult. The end of the pitch was a small but good flat ledge and I drove a piton into a sound placement. The pitch was probably the most dangerous that I have ever led. There were no good runners in a one hundred and forty foot pitch of loose difficult climbing with Tut standing at the bottom with no belay. On the crux one or two of the team pulled on the rope to save time and all three found it hard. Tut hardly remembers it now although he would have been as dead as me if I had fallen. We had most certainly been off route but an ascending traverse over mixed ground for a few pitches got us back on route. The last 200 ft to the top we managed to split into four pitches. It was the only part of the entire climb where we found some pitons. The rock was like brown sugar and by now out of our wits with fear we made a stance at every piton, all four of them. We were hoping that either one of us would take the bull by the horns and finish the thing. The top was a knife edged ridge and the only decent place to sit or lie was the point Whymper some hundreds of feet away. Graham and Murray, pre-empting such a scenario, chose to stay on the good ledge under this last buttress. We had given them a promise that we would try and throw a rope down to them in the morning so we stayed where we were and had to half sit on the sharp ridiculously exposed ridge. We could hear their petrol stove melting water and with the grip of the last few hours my throat could only croak, 'Get the stove out Tut.' He looked shame faced and said he had something really horrible to tell me like the tea bags were still in the tent. The truth was much, much worse. At the bottom of the climb he repacked his sack and the stove had been accidently left. Normally the first to moan I was shaken into silence.

We did not drink until we reached the Grande Jorasses Hut the next day having failed in our attempt to chuck the end of a 150 ft rope 200 ft to the boys. They of course got themselves up and went on to fame in NZ. That summer they had climbed the North Faces of the Eiger, Matterhorn, Piz Badile, Grande Jorrasse, Cima Grande, Le Petit Dru.

Before our holiday ended we managed to climb the Route Major on the Brenva face of Mont Blanc and the North face of the Aiguille du Dru. On this last climb we were overtaken by two Frenchmen, climbing together, very fast. Not long after, we met them again on a big ledge. They were climbing down and one of them asked had we any bandages. He held his hand up to show us—half a finger was missing and blood was everywhere. A falling stone had hit his hand whilst he was using a hand hold. Tut went green and sat down. I felt totally incompetent and impotent that we had nothing in the first aid line. The Frenchman shrugged and carried on down. Ever afterwards I carried a plaster, and two aspirins one for me and one for Tut.

# 27

## THE CAUCASUS

A trip to the Caucasus Mountains of Georgia in 1970 was only memorable for the travel and the people we met. I had had a desire to be a part of the expedition scene more for the subsidized travel than fame so for me the trip was partly successful. The Ukraine took us several days to cross, mile upon mile of wheat. The road passed through very few villages and virtually no trees. I thought of the thousands of German soldiers freezing cold, no food or petrol and a shortage of ammunition as they watched hundreds of Russian T54 tanks appear on the vast horizon as the battle of Kursk began, the vast scale of the place with nowhere to hide. For us it was easier, once in a hundred miles would be a cafe and fuel stop. Massive Russians having a shit in the communal bogs with faces like Joe Stalin, as me with the screaming shits desperately tried not to laugh at the site of them as they squatted like Sumo warriors. In the cafe there were simpletons scavenging for food from empty plates, even communist Warsaw had seemed pampered and soft by comparison. But the Russians I got drunk with and good-naturedly argued or agreed with, seemed nice people.

The mountains were big and serious with no proper system of mountain huts. Any decisions needed to be made by general consent and without any one or two of the group trying to railroad others into their particular methods or objectives. Even if in the future I had been considered for any big expeditions I would probably never have been invited, having earned a reputation for

TUT BRAITHWAITE CROSSING A NARROW SNOW BRIDGE—PAUL NUNN AND MYSELF BELAYING

CAUCAS 1970—PHOTOGRAPH BY: HAMISH MACINNES

TUT AND MYSELF NORTH FACE OF THE DRU. 1969

being a bit bolshie. At the time this truth was hard to accept and I still hankered after being in the expedition scene. The previous six years had been spent in becoming more competent for bigger and better challenges, slavishly expecting, despite being epileptic, to be invited on other peoples expeditions rather than being proactive and organising my own. Given the mortality rate of the big expeditions of the time I was probably lucky to miss the boat.

# 28

## BROKEN FEMURS

Three years of saving five pounds a week gave us the deposit for a cheap house in Glossop. The house was situated at the foot of the Snake Pass and although not that far out of Manchester I saw nothing of my old mates. However in the April me and Tut met at an ACG dinner in Wales and made arrangements to climb in the Alps together that coming summer. I frenetically set out to get fit. Easter went well. A very dry warm Glencoe was the perfect start to what should have been a successful summer. An almost dry Shibboleth with Mike Kosterlitz, Marshall's Wall, Jaywalk and Hammer with Les Brown did for my old PA rock boots. One evening back in Glossop I climbed up the inside of a Victorian factory chimney and after 4 baths I finally got clean. Another evening I had a very near miss soloing about in big boots on Shelf Benches; a crag near Glossop.

Both were the precursors for an accident. The following Wednesday evening after work me and Al Parker went over to Stanage. He had just had his shoulder operated on successfully. Seven years before we had been knocked off his motorbike, I was unhurt but Al was left with a shoulder that would dislocate with ease. He now had his arm in a sling and could not hold a rope or climb. Two years before I had backed off from soloing a climb called Millsom's Minion, that same evening I had soloed the Right Unconquerable in carpet slippers; it was a heat wave and I had been working in them. The decision I took then was that the climb looked too long a reach for me. I now decided

PETE MINKS, CLIFF PHILLIPS, ERIC JONES – NORTH FACE OF THE EIGER

PHOTOGRAPH BY: LEO DICKINSON

otherwise. After my rock boots fell apart in Glencoe I only had some that Brighams had made as an experiment three years before. Tut had thrown his pair in the dustbin, I had saved mine but they weren't much good. The crux was a thin step up which might bring a pocket within reach, it did but I was too extended to use it. Trying to reverse, I slowly fell off like a door opening. My right foot landed between two rocks, trapping it, as my body revolved my femur twisted into what the doctors described as a spiral fracture. I then bounced onto my head which precipitated a fit. When I came to, the pain was horrendous. Al thought that the fit had caused me to fall off, which was understandable but I can remember with clarity trying to reverse the move and thinking, 'Oh shit.' It was an accident of my own making, the fit happened after impact. In the early hours of the morning, with consciousness thankfully slipping away I heard the surgeon telling the assembled apprentice doctors, 'We have here an interesting case.' The next morning I asked the ward sister how long would I be in hospital, expecting at the worst a week. Three months she replied. 'OK, now tell me the truth.' Instead she looked up the line of beds and told me that a young seventeen year old at the other end of the ward would never walk again; he too had fallen off a climb on Stanage. Overcome with shame, I shut up and accepted my situation; I was put in a side ward. There was five of us, two climbers, two motor cyclists and one layabout, the craic was great. One day some kind of therapist came to visit, there did not seem any purpose to her visit except to chat, I did plenty of that, she was gorgeous and by me spinning plenty of bullshit she returned every week. The rest of the lads could safely ogle her legs which were unfortunately hidden from my view as she sat by my bed, they were chuffed to bits and would help plan the next instalment. Tut sent me several postcards, amongst his list of climbs were the North face of the Eiger, North face of the Matterhorn and the Freney Pillar on Mont Blanc, each bivouac site was marked on the pictures. Our ways had parted and he went on to greater things. After 3 month in traction I was released from Sheffield Royal hospital. You could not fault the hospital. After six weeks I fell off my bike and broke the same femur again. Two more months spent in traction, in a different hospital. The bone was refusing to completely knit so they sent me out with a calliper on my leg until it did.

# 29

## THE GLOSSOP YEARS

With hindsight breaking my leg twice, was not the disaster that it could have been. Travel to exotic places was infinitely more expensive then than in recent years. Being invited on an expedition with the attendant sponsorship was the only affordable way of climbing in distant mountain ranges. This had been a dream but in reality the pressure involved would not have suited either my health or temperament. Sometimes we come to a cross road and fate rather than choice seems to dictate the direction. I became friendly with a guy Keith Allcroft, an antique dealer who did some climbing. Whilst my leg was in a calliper I spent a lot of time with him, it was an insight into a different world. Before VAT started, the black economy was vibrant and the dealers used certain things as currency. Keith had told me what to look out for in a Grandfather clock that could affect its value. One day he stuck 900 pound in his back pocket and we went over to Yorkshire. The clock he had come to buy was everything he had told me had no value. The clock was obviously a kind of money token and as such would stay in the trade. The price paid by Keith would alter on resale as to the amount he needed in readies. It was at this time that the coal miners had brought the country to its knees and the Prime Minister Ted Heath had put the nation on a three day week, fuel was in short supply. We came across a young lad who by dint of monumental effort had felled a big hardwood tree with a small axe; it was to give to his mum for the fire. When we saw him he was stood looking at the horizontal tree with tears in his eyes as he realised that he could never chop it up into small enough pieces for a fireplace. Keith went away and came back with a big two handled saw. He sat on one side and with me still in a calliper, sitting on the other side of the tree, sawed the whole lot into fire sized logs. We delivered a third to the lads mum a third to Keith's home and a third to me and Barbara. We had ours in a big pile in the front room within easy reach of the fire. By May I was recovering. One day I walked up to Yellowslacks, a crag on the Glossop side of Bleaklow. A few years before a mad farmer had blown the crag up and with it some very good routes. After climbing on part of the remaining crag I walked over the moor and down into Longdendale across the Woodhead road and on up to Laddow rocks—a two hour walk. After doing Long climb, an 80 ft severe, I walked on past the nearly dried out Chew reservoir and down into the Chew Valley and on to Dovestones Quarry. There is a 130 ft 3 star V Diff called Waterfall climb, after climbing this I was faced with a long walk back over the empty moors. Four hours later and with the light beginning to fade, I walked into Old Glossop. A sharp pain made me think that my leg had broken again, only a few moments before I had been so euphoric. We sat up half the night worrying, the next day we found a private physiotherapist who told me that it was a part of the healing process. Barbara arranged to cycle across France with a friend in the August. The idea was for her to meet me in Chamonix after her and her friend had visited several Chateaux in the Loire valley en route. Meanwhile four of us set out in Brian Wright's Mini Van for the Kaisergebirge. A climb on the Fleishbank called the Schmuck Kamine had not had a British ascent. Geoff Douglas and my self set off for the route after arriving at midday. We roped up about three o'clock. In 1943 the famous Austrian climber Herman Bhul had a very big leader fall from the climb. The following is taken from an obituary to Marcus Schmuck in the Telegraph August 2005. '*Bhul had attempted a blank chimney on the east face of the Fleischbank in the wilder Kaiser, but had fallen; Schuck climbed it and it is still known as the Schuckkamin.'* When we arrived at the foot of the face the Asche-Luck was already in the shade. Our sweat soon becomes cold and damp, the start of the climb seemed harder and less protected than we expected and a chance to recover from the journey might have been a good idea. After a few rope lengths the Asche goes left, our route went straight up into a deep cold gorge like chimney. With some relief we found that instead of groping up the chimney our way went up a steep corner crack laced with old pitons and wooden wedges. In the event this old tat offered poor protection but often got in the way of some good hand jams. Above this pitch pitons were in short supply; worryingly, many would be ascensionists had obviously failed. We were now in the sun and some of the stances were good. The climbing had some 'unusual for limestone' off width cracks which offered poor friction for arm and leg jams but the odd good finger pockets. These holds often had the effect of pulling our bodies out of the precarious cracks rather than helping. Other pitches were superb. We arrived on the summit ridge relieved but very thirsty. The sun was a big red ball rapidly disappearing. The descent down the north ridge was at first easy but near the bottom the ridge is truncated and in the gloom we could not decide whether the route went right or left so we chose to go straight down the truncated steep wall. Two nasty abseils in near total darkness followed. After the first abseil and near the end of the rope without any back up prussic knot to stop me shooting in to space I found a small ledge about eighteen inches wide. The moon making a brief appearance enabled me to find a placement for a blade peg. Doug joined me on the ledge but with both of us pulling, the rope would scarcely move, if only we had left a karabiner on the tape sling instead of being so tight fisted. The next abseil left took me to the lip of an overhang, below was an easy bush covered ramp leading onto easy ground, but the ropes did not reach. A swing to the left might land me in a bush but once over the overhang I would have nothing for my feet to push against to initiate a pendulum. The only possibility was to run back and forth above the overhang and leaving go of the rope hoping to land in the bush before swinging back above the ramp. It worked. We arrived at the Stripsenjoch hut about midnight where the warden having heard our voices had waited up for us. Knackered we wasted the next day and despite a bad weather forecast went on the west face of the Totenkirchl the day after. Despite a damp mist we chose to climb the Peters-Eidenschink, a grade six A1 variation start to the Dulfer route. Given the need to hurry this was a daft decision. At the top of the Eidenschink the thick mist made finding our way onto the Dulfer route difficult and then the storm that had been threatening burst, the face became a waterfall preventing any possibility of abseiling down. We spent the night partly sheltered by an overhang. The following morning conditions were no different so we had to climb on through pitch after pitch of waterfalls. Back at the Stripsenjoch we left our wet gear hung on the fire escape and some of it was nicked. The area had been such a paradise 10 years before when it was not so busy. It was to be my last time in the Kaiser. Despite the place being small scale with perfect rock I had managed to turn half the routes I did there into minor epics.

South of the Brenner Pass the Dolomites still had lots of the previous winter's snow so mistakenly we carried on to Zermatt. Brian and Doug went home leaving me and Dave Ruby. Pete Alison and his brother Geoff arrived on the campsite, Geoff for some reason was not climbing so Pete came with me and Ruby to climb Lyskam by the Neruda route. On the descent Pete fell down a crevasse and burned his hand on the rope. A young French pharmacist who was camping near us bandaged Pete's hand. Peter was rather a fine specimen so as she bandaged she asked him to sleep with her—as French Pharmacist do? His brother suggested to me that if me and him got drunk we would never know whether he did or didn't and so would never let the cat out of the bag. In the event this was needless. This seemed reasonable logic so I finished the evening completely rat arsed. The next afternoon lying in the sun with a bad hangover I had a fit. That evening we set off back to the bar, passing the Bahnoff hostel, I had another fit. Madame Bina called a doctor who filled me full of barbiturate.

Years later, fit free and by then a full Guide with clients, Madame Bina looked me in the eye and said in heavily accented German 'I have seen you before, I zink.' 'No, you must be mistaken' was all I could splutter. Pete had plans for the north face of the Matterhorn but we ditched them and they gave me a lift home.

# 30

## THE FRENEY PILLAR

Things at home were well under way, Rose had made an excellent little tent and their planning was complete, then like a bad penny I rolled up. They foolishly invited me along. Barbara and Rose's leisurely holiday turned into an eight day dash across France to get back to Chamonix. When we arrived on the Biolay we ran into Pete Minks' girlfriend. On our third brew Minks and Mick Coffee came walking stiffly into view. Mick was dressed in white jeans, white clogs, dark shades on, smoking a Havana cigar, Pete was walking behind scarcely able to move he had so many, knocked off jeans under his own. Then in his thick scouse accent he uttered a sentence which I was hoping to put off for a week 'Howdy Ritch get yer gear, if we hurry up we can catch the last téléphérique' I had already been cycling most of the day but Pete was in no mood to be deflected, too many shop keepers were after him. Finding bits of my gear that various people had promised to take from Zermatt to Chamonix three weeks before was difficult, some of what I could not find I borrowed. Meanwhile Pete had got some provisions, three tubes of condensed milk a dozen tea bags two packets of powdered potatoes and soup. From the top of the cable car, down round and up the Valley Blanche was hard work and by the time we arrived at the Fourche bivi hut it was almost dark. The Central Pillar of Freney is described in the book *Im Extremen Fels*, first published in Munich in 1977, thus: '*Even in good weather the route up the Freney Pillar remains the crème de la crème of high altitude rock climbs.*' We were now only in 1972; this

THE FRENEY PILLAR

was the authors opinion five years later. For me the crux of the climb at 15,000 ft might be a problem. Having only a snack at the campsite I was already starving hungry and our sparse provisions would not allow a feast. After the col Moore, the way descends on to the Brenva Glacier and then ascends the north east couloirs of the Col de Peuterey, a climb of 550 m and D- in its own right. I had borrowed a long straight ice axe. We took a long time and by the time we reached the col a cloud covered the top of the Aiguille Blanche like a cowl and bad weather was looking imminent. Somebody had made a really good ice cave and after a brew inside it was tempting to stay there but as Pete observed if the next morning dawned fine we would have wished we had have gone as far the start of the Pillar. Once at a bivi site it was snowing and we had visions of Walter Bonatti's epic retreat in 1961, which was only eleven years before. Then only three of seven climbers survived, some of the cream of European alpinism snuffed out in the extreme weather they encountered. We need not have worried, the next morning dawned fine and by the time it started to snow again we were under the Chandelle only about 250 m from the finish on the Brouillard ridge. Sitting discarded on a ledge was a large packet of bacon. Two pitches below the top of the Chandelle we made a bivi on a decent ledge. The next morning dawned fine but cold. Pete spewed his bacon up before we left the ledge. We should have sat about for an hour to let the sun melt the verglas. The final two pitches were iced up and we had a tricky lead each. On the summit of Mont Blanc we met two German climbers, one had stuck a crampon in his leg and covered in purple antiseptic was a neat hole. Pete, despite his devil may care attitude, had a very good first aid kit with some strong pain killers complete with syringe. Muttering something about the war he shot off down the Bosses ridge. Down at the Gouter hut a French Guide, who Pete vaguely knew, gave us some of his clients food, we stayed far too long talking and had to walk the last part of the descent through a pitch dark forest. Once

PETE MINKS PREPARING TO BIVI, CENTRAL PILLAR OF FRENEY, MONT BLANC 1972

on the road we stuck our thumbs out and a French lad gave us a lift into Cham. Unfortunately I only did that one climb in the Alps with Pete. On the hill there are few people I would sooner be with.

AUTHOR LOOKING UP TO THE FRENEY PILLARS FROM THE SOUTH RIDGE OF THE AIGUILLE

NOIRE DE PEUTEREY 1990—PHOTOGRAPH BY: DAVE TIDMARSH

ME AND BARBARA YOSEMITE 1973

PHOTOGRAPH BY: PAUL ROSS

# 31

## 1973 YOSEMITE VALLEY

After several pints in the pub Geoff Morgan suggested a trip to
Yosemite to climb El Capitan. Cost would be a problem, driving
to the Alps in old bangers was not financially that expensive
and camping in Chamonix was free. California was a long way
and air travel was expensive. Expeditions to obscure mountain
ranges could often obtain financial sponsorship but individual
schemes had to be self financing. My lack of speed prevented me
earning much bonus which kept my wage at flat rate. Serving an
apprenticeship on the corporation is good for problem solving
and drinking tea but not for speed. Re-enter Keith Allcroft. He
had observed the huge amounts of hardwoods that got trashed
when old buildings were either being refurbished or demolished.
Tropical hardwood often in four foot widths cut from the jungles
of Malaya in the heyday of the British Empire; in a different
value system this timber would be priceless. Keith agreed with
this sentiment and set about doing the world a favour. Most
drawer units either in offices or for holding textile merchandise
had a hard wood top, one inch thick between three or four foot
wide, long straight grained pieces of mahogany cut from huge
trees. The renovation firms or the demolition men did not see
the value of the wood, nor, I suppose, did they know how or
where to sell it. Keith and his merry helpers would move in
and remove the stuff. Where a building was being refurbished
it was doing the owners a favour although they did not know
it. I was working on a new housing scheme and the foreman
did not object to my having the odd day or two off. Helping

Keith save the planet was profitable and paid the air fare for myself and Barbara to Canada. Another little money earner that appeared was a precursor to a vast industry that would, a few years later, help to keep hordes of unemployable crag rats off the dole. The deal was that Arthur Robinson had given up hod carrying bricks for a living, having knackered his back. He was now working for a scaffolding company pricing jobs. Salford cathedral had just been stone cleaned and silicone stuff squirted on it to protect the stone. However, the guy who was supposed to spray the liquid on the actual spire bit on the Sunday got drunk instead and rolled in late on the Monday by which time the scaffold had been dropped, leaving the last fifty feet exposed. Me and Billy Birch took two days off work and using a chisel to rake out the occasional joints, inserted pitons for aid. A series of abseil descents with a spray canister in a rucksack did the job. We went with Arthur to get paid. I was expecting a backhander in a site cabin but instead we were ushered into a posh office in a proper office block. A guy with a serious feeling of gravitas about him was sat poised over a cheque book, pen in hand, 'How much money do you require for the job Mr Robinson?' Arthur replied 'Will sixty quid be too much?' I could have strangled him, the man was obviously prepared to pay a lot more and I could see our Yosemite trip paid for. But a longer term consideration which neither Arthur nor me had the vision to see was the huge business opportunity which had presented itself; industrial rope access before anyone else.

In Vancouver I had several friends from the old Langdale crowd who had moved out there to live in the nineteen sixties. They relaxed by smoking cannabis, listening to the Moody Blues and awaiting the eventual death of capitalism. Pete Shotton, his wife Joan and their kids were planning a trip to New Mexico to make blood brothers of the Hopi Indians and offered us a lift to Yosemite. It was a squeeze in their VW Van. Alan Dewison and Morgan had gone on ahead by Greyhound bus, not as much fun as our Steinbeck adventure. In the dark Pete took the wrong turning and got lost, tired out we tumbled out of his van and slept under the trees. The night was cold and we were obviously higher than the valley so the dawn was welcome. Nobody had mentioned the blue Jays, but after a while the novelty of watching these comic blue and black birds wore off and I rolled over onto my stomach. We were on the rim of the Yosemite Valley looking down and across at Half Dome. From our vantage point the slabby side of the huge Dome of granite was facing me and appeared impossibly steep and utterly blank, and my heart sank. It seemed that drunken hubris when hatching this trip had got me totally out of my depth. Little did I know that before we left Yosemite Barbara and I would climb that slab of rock up a very reasonably graded superb climb called Snake Dike.

Camp four was full of climbers, the odd bear and thieving racoons. Everybody stored food in sacks and pulled them into the trees out of the way of the animals. After a few days we thought the bears were a myth and left the haul sack of food on the floor. I had arranged to go doing a climb on Sentinel rock with a very good American climber, Steve Wunch. In the middle of the night Barbara shot up shouting 'Bear! A bear!' We pulled the sack up a tree and went back to bed. Just after dawn we crawled out of the tent to make a brew and as I undid the knot securing the sack, the bear along with a coyote, silhouetted against the sky line, was just beginning to stand up. After shouting and throwing stones they left. Steve arrived. He wanted to do the Salethe Steck route on Sentinel Rock without using any nuts. The crux is a tight squeeze chimney. Lying on a ledge at the foot of the chimney I found an Hexentric which was the perfect size for the crack. This was the first time I had seen one. It was a new piece of kit on the market. Steve was not against me using it for protection but he refused to use it when he was leading. For me to find it when it was most

EL CAPITAN, YOSEMITE

PHOTOGRAPH BY: PAUL ROSS

ON MAMMOTH LEDGE WITH PAUL ROSS, SALETHE WALL, EL CAPITAN. YOSEMITE 1973

PHOTOGRAPH BY: GEORGE HOMER

needed was a miracle. Most of the climb we did without any pitons or nuts and it was quite dangerous. I was on a learning curve, beware of bears and American hot shots, both nice but dangerous. The next day I ran into Paul Ross. The place was full of British climbers, camp four was free and in some respects the place was like the old Biolay campsite in Chamonix, except for a few pluses. The Americans were in the main very friendly, the climate was usually hot and sunny without being humid and with very little effort you could be climbing on perfect granite, with magnificent trees all around and exotic animals wandering about the place, it was heaven. The Merced River was full of snow melt from the high country and was too cold to swim in and the campsite was not well supplied with showers or shops but that was the only down side. Pete Minks was on the campsite and had done an ascent of Salathe wall on El Capitan with an Australian, Rick White. Doug Scott had made the first British ascent with the equally famous Austrian climber Peter Haebler. The route still needed a completely British ascent. Ross had worked this little known fact out and looking around for his team found me and George Homer. George was a laconic scouser who looked like a cross between a gun slinger and a hippy. Like most scousers he had a good sense of humour and was a sound guy. Him and Paul both smoked dope, so our ascent of Salathe Wall was not fast, in fact it took five days. We had a huge haul sack which contained water, sleeping bags, a hammock belonging to George and a big bag of Gorp. This was an American invention and consisted of salted peanuts and chocolate smarties. The cannabis was extra. El Cap is about 3,400 feet and 35 pitches long. At the time the climb was about 50% free and 50% artificial climbing. Todd Skinner did the first free ascent in 1988. Paul's plan was that I did the free climbing and George would do the artificial climbing, meanwhile he would jummer up each pitch taking pictures. This plan nearly worked but we did get him to lead three pitches. Paul was one of the best Lake District climbers of his generation but at the time he had grown idle. In old age he became a fitness fanatic and lost his sense of humour. He did get some amazing slides for which I was very grateful. The second day went quickly, we had slept the first night comfortably on Heart ledge and took ages to get going. After a couple of pitches the line of weakness we had been following ran out. On our left was a steep blank wall bounded a long way over to the left with a long right facing crack which is called the Hollow flake. To reach this crack involved climbing fifty feet above the belay then being lowered thirty feet before running backwards and forwards in a pendulum until you can throw yourself into the crack, attempt to stay there and then climb it. The whole enterprise is made harder by a groove that you have to jump over. Having failed to get a lodgement the first time I went sliding back across the wall. The second time of trying I got my foot in the crack and pulled myself precariously in. This manoeuvre was helped by having boots on, for most of the climb rock shoes would have been much better but for once boots were. Under a feature called El Cap spire there is another very good ledge but one pitch below it, it went dark. George had a purpose made hammock, Paul had a nylon flysheet off an old tent and I hung in my harness all night. Paul's flysheet stretched until he was sat on my head, he claimed that in the dark it was dodgy untying knots so we remained like that until dawn. Two days later George had nailed up the overhanging head wall and from the last of the aid points hand traversed right to a narrow ledge. I was last and it was going dark when I had to stop jummaring, remove the last piton and free climb the traverse. Shouting for them to take in the rope was hopeless as they were on their second joint, so with 150 ft of slack rope I did the traverse. The ledge was shaped like a gutter, it was possible to lie in it completely secure. In the middle of the ledge the lip of the gutter disappears for about 18 inches where water has worn an exit. Paul was sat with his legs dangling over the void a joint in his fingers George was jammed tight in the gutter in his sleeping bag. My side of the gutter was still free so without a word of complaint about them not taking the rope in, I got in my sleeping bag. With me and George secure, Paul who had finished smoking his joint realised his mistake and spent a rough night sitting upright. The last pitch was really good, after thrutching up a crack you go out onto a wall with chicken heads making big holds, feeling secure and euphoric I could look down at the Merced River over three thousand feet below. On the top we left the haul sack and most of the gear in a dead tree hoping to collect it later and set off for the valley. Paul got us lost but was determined he knew the way. There was no point in arguing, we had had a brilliant time without a wrong word, all that mattered was finding water. Down at camp four some American guys had brewed some beer to celebrate our return. The four of them had packed in good jobs in San Francisco and become middle aged hippies. Paul had a climbing shop in New Hampshire so most of the gear in the dead tree was his, he told me and George to split it between us and he went back East. After some more routes it was nearly time to go home. Barbara had started climbing that year with me but my being obsessed with El Cap meant that we had not yet done a route together in Yosemite. Snake Dike on Half Dome would be a really good finish to our holiday. To reach the foot of the route entails a long walk into a hanging side valley called Little Yosemite. The feel of the place is kind of Alpine, grassy with trees dotted about like a heavenly park. To save weight we borrowed a nine millimetre rope off Alan but he never thought to say it was short and although bolt protected, the belays are 160 ft apart with one rusty bolt runner per pitch. On every pitch Barbara had to start climbing before I could get to the next belay. The climb gets its name from a narrow band of quartz running for hundreds of feet up an otherwise steep blank slab and was formed where the softer granite has been eroded from either side of the quartz. The climb ends where the angle changes, conveniently by a solitary old tree lost in a sea of granite. A very exposed walk up easy slabs ends on a massive flat summit. The descent is down a series of cables and chunks of wood, after which we walked and ran, hoping to catch the last shuttle bus to keep a dinner date with an American couple we had met. On the Greyhound bus going back to Vancouver was a young guy blowing aimlessly into a mouth organ, mile after mile but nobody told him to shut up. Somebody got on the bus and sat next to him, he told the newcomer, 'That was my own comp-o-sition.' The guy, instead of telling him to shut up said, 'Yes very nice.' It all seemed so tolerant and friendly. Years later when the kids were grown up me and Barbara went for a trip to Toulomne Meadows which is a place full of granite domes near Yosemite, at a higher elevation. We had a good time climbing but apart from a couple of New Englanders we met on the North West face of Fairview Dome nobody was that friendly. Maybe that love and peace thing of the sixties and early seventies really did work, who knows but our trip in '73 was great and it was where our first son was conceived, amazing what a bit of sun can do.

ON THE SUMMIT OF EL CAPITAN WITH PAUL ROSS AND GEORGE HOMER 1973

PHOTOGRAPH BY: GEORGE HOMER

# 32

## HIMALAYA

I suppose the first sign was when she cried instead of shouting for me to stop talking and take the blinking rope in. Then the next morning she came to the station to wave me off to the Himalaya dressed in black, with a furry black hat on her head, shades of Julie Christy in Dr Zhivago. She was pregnant but never said; if only she had. The expedition leader never discussed money, only a nominal amount was asked for at the time. The presumption being that the lecture circuit would pay the rest when we got home. After Yosemite in May, a trip to the Alps in the summer would have been great but that required money. An offer to join an expedition to the Himalaya seemed like a freebie. I did not know any of the other members of the team, so I got them to ask Alan Dewison along. As the time to go got nearer, I became aware that the money was a mirage and only consisted of a bank loan. Worse even than the lack of money was that I and some other members of the trip would definitely not get on with each other. We flew out in separate groups. Our plane had to make an unscheduled stop in Bombay because of a storm in central India. We were ferried across the city in buses and taxis to wait out the delay. The opulence of the hotel was obscene. Set against the dreadful poverty that I had observed from the taxi, it seemed disgusting that I was doing nothing more important than risking life and limb trying to climb a mountain. Alan Dewison and Alan Fyffe had gone to Bombay to get our equipment off a ship and bring it by public transport to Nepal. The monsoon lasted longer than normal and the ship's captain was reluctant to open the hold because his cargo would get wet. The two Alan's had to wait for ages for the gear, negotiate several bus journeys and help dig through several washed out roads, this resulted in the equipment arriving a month late. Four of us had already set out as an advance guard. We arrived near the mountain with no gear no tea and only white rice and a little dhal for food. It was pouring down when we emerged from the jungle. High angled grass and other vegetation ran to the foot of an enormous face of steep rotten rock which appeared to have a flat icy top. Over to our right the face was punctuated by a glacier river issuing out of steep jungle, to the left the face ran on, flanking the side of the valley. This ugly spectacle was so different than my idea of a Himalayan giant where white peaks float majestically in the air surrounded by snow white glaciers. In truth what we were camped under was a giant barrier which stood away from the big peaks of the Dhaulagiri chain. With no mountaineering gear our time could have been used very productively building a good base camp and exploring the area. The river I mentioned previously must have started from a glacier not far out of our sight, finding this glacier might possibly have given us access to the peaks without having to climb the 5000 ft obstacle of decomposing granite. I was never going to have the chance to find out. Ian Rowe persisted in his opinion that to gain access to our peak we would have to first climb this barrier. We could have camped just above the tree line and this would have given us easy access to firewood. There was also a bamboo framework of a building that a Japanese expedition had left behind. Instead Ian had us camp on a moraine hard up against the barrier. This involved the kitchen boys having to drag fire wood up at least 1,500 ft of ascent to cook the glutinous white rice and thimble full of dhal we had twice a day. After eight days of lying in a soaking wet tent on a pile of stones and with no real nutrition I had a fit. This situation became serious as I continued having fits, only briefly becoming conscious between each one. The circumstances that had produced this state of affairs proved difficult to improve, hypothermia, lack of extra medication, food and ironically thirst. The porters had made a rough stone shelter for themselves, they cooked on a fire. Eventually I came around sufficiently to drink some warm water. Proximity to their much enlarged fire had helped me to become drier and if not warm I was no longer shivering and fitting. We had been holding onto a small amount of real food for emergencies so we now shared a good meal. The experience had been horrible, any chance of my continuing with the expedition were nil so the next day Ian Rowe kindly accompanied me back to Pokhara. On our five day journey the rain had stopped and the sun came out, we could buy food and tea in the many tea houses and I walked into Pokhara fit and well. Both of the Alan's had appeared with the gear. Me and Alan Dewison shared a tent. His news from home was a pleasant shock, Barbara was pregnant. Like me, Alan had not previously known any of the other expedition members and he implored me to come back to the mountain with him; given the circumstances there was no way I could do. It was the last time I saw him, he was killed six weeks later. A gentle soul, he would do no one any harm. Weeks of good weather had allowed the expedition to climb the giant barrier from where there was a good view of the proposed peak on the other side of a glacier. Camp six was established on this glacier on the same altitude as camp one. From camp six Alan and Tony attempted the peak, Alan fell to his death. One of the kitchen boys was killed in an avalanche when they were stripping Camp One. Back in the UK the expedition left us all with a debt to pay, as the proposed lecture tour would have only been possible if the peak had been climbed. I had been lucky but the experience scarred my mind like no other. A statistic often quoted at the time was that a climber taking part in a Himalayan expedition had a 10% chance of being killed. Not exactly a sport, more like war; definitely not for me.

THE ECKPFEILER, MONT BLANC

# 33

## 1974 FATHERHOOD, THE ECKPFEILER
## AND A CHANGE OF DIRECTION

I telephoned the hospital on my way home from work. My head ached from balancing 8x4 sheets of plaster board, having spent the day covering the walls and ceilings of a new house. Elated I caught the bus to Ashton. Barbara was in Ashton infirmary having just given birth to our first son. He arrived already full of enthusiasm and we called him Ian. A week later they were home and doing fine so I kept to an arrangement I had made with Billy Birch and John Yates to climb on Ben Nevis for a week. Guilt at leaving Barbara and a baby Ian behind gave me the determination to make our long planned visit worthwhile so before ascending to the CIC hut and against our agnostic belief I suggested we pray, like with our hands and eyes shut for good weather, and for all the piss taking it worked in spectacular fashion. We climbed a totally banked out Gardyloo Gully and then over a four day period on a bone dry Carn Dearg: Toro – E2 5c, Centurion – HVS 5a, The Bat – E2 5b, and Sassenach – E1 5a. The reality of having a family and some sense of responsibility had not yet sunk in. A very keen and capable alpinist called John Wilkinson kindly offered us a lift to the Alps, with no fixed time for a return this proved to be a mistake. After a visit to the Engelhorner and Zermatt we again ended up in a wet Chamonix. A week or so later I ran into a German climber I knew Reinhardt Karl, he said the forecast was good for two days and he was heading for the Fourche hut and the Freney Pillar. Me and John Yates had just done the North Face of the Plan, a classic TD ice route of 1000 m. If the weather remained indifferent we might not manage to achieve anything else so we followed Reinhardt up to the Fourche Hut heading for the Bonnati Gobbi route on the Eckpfeiler Buttress. This is on the Italian side of Mont Blanc. The start of the climb is at 3400 metres it finishes on the Peuterey ridge at 4,250 m and then follows this to finish at 4,807 m on the summit. The grade for individual pitches is not technically hard, however the climb is long and in places very loose and would be difficult to retreat from in case of injury or bad weather. These kind of climbs were considered to be good training for the Greater Ranges but in truth they were bloody horrible. Our ascent of the Salathe wall on El Cap the year before was infinitely more demanding but safer and enjoyable with rescue possible, unlike the remote Eckpfeiler Buttress. Such big mountain routes have to be climbed in big boots, rucksacks holding a stove, food, bivi sheet, extra clothes and ice climbing gear. I think this kind of climbing is no longer mainstream. Near the top of the rock section were three long unprotected pitches, two of them were my leads. The Croz spur and the Phillip Flam had looser sections, but those sections were not as long. I found myself talking to holds, praying for them not to give way. Above followed a few pitches of steep ice which were cold and in the shadow. A tension traverse left, from an ice screw, enabled us to get off the ice and onto a big flat ledge still warm from the afternoon sun. Above us were hundreds of feet of mixed climbing leading up to the finish of the buttress on the Peuterey ridge. We only melted sufficient water for some soup and one brew but none for the morning. At first it was nice to sit watching the lights twinkling in Courmayeur but once it became cold we pulled the bivi sack over our heads and fell asleep. The sack was black and so we never saw the dawn, it was only the heat from the sun that woke us up. Neither of us had a watch and convinced the day was half way through we rushed off without a drink. As the day passed thirst and altitude made us go slower and slower. Eventually a pair of alpinists doing the Peuterey ridge caught us up at the final cornice, we left an ice screw belay in place for them and moved onto the easy ground leading to the summit. Cloud was gathering and was beginning to restrict visibility. Two German lads who had just exited from the Freney Pillar were having trouble getting a fix on the summit. One of them was looking at a map, upside down, whilst his mate had gone across to some rocks to improve his view. I had been here with Minks two years before and knew it was not far but with visions of my epic in 1966 I was becoming nervous with the worsening weather. A shout of 'Gipfel' from the German lad signalled that he had had a brief glimpse of the summit. I started to run across before it disappeared from view. Blunt crampons on hard ice need a positive stamp but at a run I slipped and went off down a snowfield which disappeared into an abyss ultimately heading thousands of feet toward the valley. Trying to break on the icy slope was futile; it would be ironic to kill us both from such easy ground. The rope was uncoiled on the floor by John's feet, he could only briefly watch before he was pulled off. After a few hundred feet I became airborne, flew over a bergshrund and landed in soft snow underneath. I would probably have continued but John landed on top of me pushing me into the snow and giving him a hand hold on my body. It was now going dark and the French alpinists had taken the German lads into their care. They kindly shouted down that they would wait for us and that they knew the way. Shook up, we foolishly declined and pulled the bivi sheet over our heads. Late the following day the bad weather relented and we made it to the Vallot hut. In the night two Serbian lads appeared. They had been behind us on the climb but still had some food left which they shared with us.

It was another week of rain and cold wind before Dave gave us a lift home. Dave 'Wilko' Wilkinson is every inch a true mountaineer, happy with the masochistic dangerous environment of big mountains. I, by comparison liked dipping my toes into them to make simple pursuits seem better. Life in a tent for Barbara with a three month old Ian had been an ordeal, for a time he had appeared ill, back in Glossop she had him at the doctors before we even got home. The Doctor examined them both and said 'The baby is alright but I will give you a prescription for Valium.' The Valium went down the nearest grid. The Eckpfeiler was to be my last Grand Course which entailed at least one night out, no more looking up at a star filled sky from a bivouac on some ledge wondering what we were doing there, or weeks spent on free campsites with no facilities. Over the next ten or twenty years the weather in the Alps definitely became warmer and drier, the Mer de Glace has now shrunk beyond recognition. Every good quality lump of granite has sprouted bolted climbs of amazing quality and the emphasis on big mixed climbs has lessened.

In the years before leaving Glossop in 1975, one particular day stands out. It had its origins a week or two before in Stoney Middleton cafe. Tom Proctor and Geoff Birtles had been trying a line left of Tom's route Green Death, on Millstone Edge. They told me and Billy Birch how they intended digging a big hole underneath the line so that the one and only peg placement might prevent landing on the floor. That they had been so upfront in telling us about all this implied that they did not consider us capable of doing it. Billy got sick of my ranting on and said 'Right! We will do it.' The following Saturday morning Billy with me and Gabriel Regan rolled up at Millstone. Gabe ran into a couple of his mates John Allen and Steve Bancroft. These three plus Gabriel's mate James Moran became leading lights of their generation. Billy went off to abseil the line. Scared at what I had now let myself in for I went for a shit. Near the top Billy found a placement for a small blade peg, it went in with a slight knock about half an inch, utterly useless. It was also out of reach so he left a sling clipped to it. Lower down he placed an angle peg in the shot hole. Many new climbs of the period were inspected on a top rope, but I thought this was against the grain and decided that I would lead it with no prior inspection. Pre-placing protection was bad enough. The climbing soon became thin and technical. Tom Proctor was one of the best climbers of his generation and even he was having second thoughts about leading it, even though he had previously top roped the line. Given that Tom was a much better climber than I was the chance of me finding a move physically impossible was a possibility. The crux came at 70 ft which was just below the top and comprised of a scoop that ended the sharp arête. The shot hole peg was now far below and useless, the ground flat and stony. The blade peg was utterly useless. My first attempt at the crux failed and I had to make a very tenuous retreat to the good foothold. On this first attempt I had managed to get my knee into the bottom of a scoop but my South Sea Bubble jeans lacked sufficient friction. On the next attempt I would need to get my toe into the same place but once committed to this move it would be impossible to reverse. Above the scoop was an obvious feature carved in the rock at the very top of the climb but having stood up could I reach it? The abseil ropes were only twenty feet round the corner, the temptation to cheat was immense but for now I could stand on a good foothold and weigh the odds, or summon up the courage to go for it. This is what is at the heart of climbing, a finely balanced judgement when at times like this there is no second chance. Using small side holds I moved up into the scoop, stood up and reached the jug. Years later I met Steve Bancroft in Chamonix, he was busking around Europe. Steve told me it was an impressively brave show. I bought him another beer but forgot to tell him that it was bravado and fear of loss of face more than courage. All the boys seconded the climb and agreed on its great quality. In the present guide book Edge Lane is graded E5 5c hardly difficult in the modern era but still a bold lead. What made the day so special was the company of the next generation, a day to remember and a day to remember Derbyshire by.

END OF PART ONE

PART TWO

# 34

## SCOTLAND

In the summer of 1971 in between getting out of hospital and breaking my femur a second time, a friend Neil Parker took me and Barbara a ride around Scotland for a holiday. We visited Pat Walsh and his wife Pat at their croft on the Isle of Skye. With deteriorating eyesight Pat's climbing years were behind him. He was working his croft, building houses for other people and dabbling in the stock market. The sight of a rough looking Glaswegian staring through bottle top glasses at the Financial Times was bizarre, the idea that he knew what he was looking at even more so, but he did. Pat fancied expanding his building work but needed a finishing joiner. We also found that grants might be available which could help Barbara start a pottery. With Pat's offer of some work we took a chance and bought the feu on three acres of croft land that had permission for a house to be built on it. Four years later we had gone off the idea when a letter arrived from the Crofters Commission. It was a directive to tell us that if we did not want the land somebody else would. It was make our mind up time, maybe a visit north to talk them into giving us more time to think would be a good idea. The weather was fantastic, the Isle Skye was bathed in winter sun, the sea like a mill pond. In Inverness the Crofters Commission was no problem but the HIDB did not seem keen on giving grants to people with no real collateral of their own, although they did find me a job. It was at a place making pine furniture near Cromarty. The idea being to move to the East coast, until we had at least started to build a house on our croft. Unfortunately this job was another one of their failed business plans and when I arrived the other employees had gone and the electricity was cut off. The business man behind the scheme lived in Edinburgh. After getting the electric back on he paid me for a year, making furniture out of his fabulous stock of Scots Pine. The business was in liquidation but it was in the period before the liquidators moved in. With a foreman around I would not have lasted a day but over the course of time I became competent and had a wonderful year. The building had been a school presumably still owned by the council. One day a man appeared, ostensibly to check on the fabric of the place, after several brews and a two hour talk he put me on to a friend of his who was thinking of opening a pottery behind his Hotel in Dingwall. Billy Deas bought the gear and set Barbara up, she had six years of fun making and running her own pottery until she decided to go back teaching so that she could have the same holidays as the boys. After the furniture operation closed down I was owed back wages, the local shop had let us run up a lot of credit so I went working as casual labour unloading ships in Invergordon. On the second day I broke my forearm, and when the plaster was removed my elbow would not straighten, which left both my elbows in the same state.

At this time there were only a few easily accessible crags in the north of Scotland, the emphasis was on 'The Hill'. Brownie points were earned by being a competent all rounder i.e. A phantom hill walker, grade 3 snow / ice climber and rock climbing only on mountain crags, the longer the walk to the crag the more brownie points. That first summer, climbing with two new friends Peter McDonald and Dave Jenkins, we climbed The Needle and The Steeple on the magnificent Shelter Stone, a nine hundred foot face of perfect granite. We also did a new climb on Sgurr an Fhidhleir six hundred foot long. These were long superb climbs in remote positions. The next summer, nineteen seventy six, was marvellous weather and our next son Alan was born. I was working locally for Macrae's builders doing a council estate up. I had also teamed up with the infamous John MacLean of the Creagh Dhu. We had good trips into Carnmore and the Dubh Loch and several new climbs on Beinn Eighe. After two years I had a day on Stanage on my own, I was surprised how hard gritstone now felt. At home the lack of small crags to visit easily and not just in a period of dry weather was showing its effect. Meanwhile in Ross-shire Viscount Tarbet and his friend Bob Brown would before long set about cleaning and climbing every overgrown crag in the area and did everyone a favour.

Our new location made winter climbing easy to access. Previously I had only ever made the trip to Scotland about twice in winter. Chopping steps up vertical or sometimes overhanging ice with an ordinary straight picked ice axe is strenuous, dangerous and requires a cool disposition. The standard of climbs in Scotland done with such gear is amazing. I soon ditched my old gear and bought two Terrordactyl ice tools; they were truly amazing, it was like having two good handholds all the time. They transformed ice climbing forever. Hamish MacInnes who invented them must have had the old school spitting feathers; all that balancing about in a freezing gale, fingers crimped in chopped little nicks in the ice while crampons were scratching about, it was the equivalent of inventing a bionic hand for rock climbing. For chickens these new ice tools were superb, I was chuffed to bits.

Now I had them I had to try them out. Creag Meagaidh seemed a good plan, somewhere new. After a two hour walk I stood looking at the crag working out the different lines, cloud obscured the top of the crag but the first three quarters of a climb called Pumpkin was visible and looked good. The new ice tools worked a treat one steep section after another. I climbed with unusual ease but always the following section would still look desperate. It would take ages to adjust to a world where steep ice could be climbed with relative ease. The Terrordactyls did have draw backs—they were a little bit too short which often

USING DROPPED ICE TOOLS CLIMBING CASCADE, STAG ROCKS, CAIRNGORMS 1981

PHOTOGRAPH BY: PETER CLIFF

meant sore knuckles, and the pick angled down too steeply which required a pronounced downward motion. This could make moving onto easy ground difficult, whereas a swing of an old axe could get more purchase. Topping out from Pumpkin into the cloud and finding the descent would have been more of a problem than the climb, but then out of the mist appeared two young Scots. I did not need to ask them the way, merely to be friendly and follow them. Andy Nesbit became the most prolific winter new router of his generation and is still doing new climbs thirty five years later. Alf Robertson eventually moved to Spain. In the next few years I enjoyed climbing with both of them. After a good Sunday on Ben Nevis with Peter McDonald, Pete left me in the CIC hut and went home to work. The crag was in amazingly good condition. At the time Zero gully was still rated as a difficult climb but was now banked out with snow / ice rather than straight water ice. With every placement I made the pick of my Terrordactyl sank all the way in. The crag was devoid of people and the silence and cold gave a feeling of menace but with the crux behind me nothing could go wrong. The upper gully should have been a cruise but then I came to a steep wall of ice only about fifteen feet high. Because it took me by surprise I saw it with a different mindset, forgetting that I had mobile jugs in my hands. Compared with lower down, this wall was insignificant but already spooked by the silence my hubristic confidence evaporated. I placed an ice screw clipped a large loop of rope into it and easily climbed the wall. To abandon the screw seemed a waste. Without any obvious belay a horizontally buried Terrordactyl in the soft snow might hold my weight so I gingerly abseiled down for the screw. Going back up with one tool was a problem, pulling on the rope with one hand my body would sway from the ice which made it nearly impossible to get a placement with the ice tool held in my other hand. Amazing how the belay held but above the climbing was straight forward and from the summit there was three hundred and sixty degree view of the many hundreds of peaks of my new home bathed in a blue sky. Later when I was stood hitching hiking home Mac Innes pulled in for petrol, I never mentioned the trick with the buried ice tool. He might have included it in his next mountain rescue training manual.

# 35

## CORNICE PROBLEMS

Cornices don't always form in the same place and are seldom found on Stanage.

MacLean had bought one good ice tool and new crampons. For his other hand, he genuinely had a slaters pick; at the time he was working as a slater. After a long night in the pub and a party we got to bed by five a.m. – still drunk we were on our way up the Ben by eight. January days are short and this one was also very cold. Point five Gully is a thousand foot runnel of ice, a grade five ultra classic deserving of a team buzzing with competence. Once at the top of the climb a full moon was out but fearing that it might become obscured by cloud we rushed off to find the descent gully. We had neither untied nor coiled the ropes but had enormous coils of rope wrapped willy-nilly around our necks. 'Here we are' I shouted, delighted by my knowledge, 'Number four gully' and with that I walked over the cornice. John saw me disappear and fell on his back hoping to hold me, as the rope came tight around my neck I stopped, snow and rope sharing my weight. Having prevented me from sliding off down the gully it would have seemed sensible for John to untie and look for a different way down but then framed against the moon he appeared in mid air like a huge black bat. He just thought, 'Bugger it' and jumped. Luckily the gully was filled with soft snow.

On the easiest or hardest winter climbs cornices can be the sting in the tail.

A year later and slightly more competent I had arranged to meet Andrew Nesbit under the Shelter Stone. The walk in started from a deserted Coire Cas, in the moonlight the ski lifts had an air of menace that accentuated the loneliness. In the true wilderness beyond, the emptiness felt safe, the only danger would be self made. After walking along a frozen Loch Avon, crossing the river which flowed into it was a dodgier affair but once across I soon found the cave under a huge boulder, our shelter for the weekend. I soon had the primus stove melting snow hoping Andrew would arrive in time for the first brew. Almost on demand his head torch appeared as he too walked along the frozen Loch. He had driven from Aberdeen after work. I had only driven from Inverness. The following morning the weather was perfect but we would have to spend most of the day in the shade. Over to the left of the Shelter Stone was the huge bulk of Carn Etchachan and our proposed climb; Scorpion, grade five, 240 m. Until the last pitch the climbing was sustained but enclosed and with enough scraping and searching a runner or belay could be found. Above this section we came to a snow slope leading up to a gigantic cornice. Far out to the left the cornice petered out into some rocks. To miss the challenge and not grab the scorpion by the tail seemed a cop out so I headed for the cornice. The nearer I got the bigger the cornice appeared but by now I was kicking steps through a hard crust and into soft snow, retreat down this would be impossibly dangerous. Maybe once under the cornice it might be possible to place an ice screw. In the event I got a blade peg in a shallow crack; but with only half an inch of purchase it was useless. With no chance of abseiling down I would have to go for it. Up close there was not one bulge to climb but two, however some rock peeking through might provide a foothold. Terrordactyls had a bucket shaped adze, useless for chopping steps but good for a placement in soft snow. With my feet under a bulge I made progress by pulling with my left tool in a strip of ice and alternating with my right tool using the adze in snow to pull and hold most of my weight. Well in excess of a hundred foot below Andrew was well belayed but with no protection between us a fall would have taken me that distance and the same again, giving neither of us a chance. The adze placement held for two moves before I could pull over the bulge and bridge my left foot across to the rock. The next bulge was not as big or overhanging but was all soft snow. This required using the shafts of the tools and a desperate thrash. Poised before making the effort life seemed so unjust, having arrived here so near the top to be confronted by this. Just luck and speed, not skill or strength would prevail. The top was flat and sunny but with nothing to belay on. Andrew seconding could not afford to fall or fail. The next day we did a three star climb on Carn Etchachan, safely. Walking back down Coire Cas in the afternoon was pleasant... There were people and children happily skiing.

The break off point of a cornice is influenced by the ground underneath and can be much further back from the edge than is obvious.

We had had a very good winter, Easter was late and although there was voluminous amounts of snow on the hills the mild damp weather had started to soften the snow. The winter climbing season was over but we had arranged to meet Dick Renshaw at a small bothie, miles away from anywhere. On the way in we spent a night at the Sinclair hut. This was one of the many bothies in the Cairngorms that were knocked down several years later on the bizarre grounds that people used them. An easy climb the following morning confirmed the obvious; the snow pack was becoming unconsolidated, wet and heavy. The huge cornices were ready to collapse. By the time Dick arrived at the Garbh Coire bothie there was already eight of us in a place only big enough for three. Dick had walked all the way from Braemar, miles and miles through the snow in hush puppy shoes with his mountain boots in his rucksack. This was not some weird fetish that he had but because he had had some toes amputated not long before. It would not be unfair to say that Andrew and Dick made an impressive pair of masochists so after a horrendous night in the bothie they had ambitions. As we parted company Andrew muttered a warning about cornices, it seemed unnecessary; visibility was good. The climb I had chosen finished by traversing right a few hundred feet above where Andy and Dick were scraping about on a steep rock wall. In reasonable conditions my route would have been easy but the snow was wet deep and dangerous although happily the exit had no cornice. The summit of Braeriach was not so far away but it was now snowing with thick mist and a strong wind blowing spindrift about. Trying to find a descent through the barrier of cornices took precedence over bagging a summit. At first I walked parallel to the cornice but fifty or sixty feet away from the edge. Going any nearer might risk being the trigger to collapse the huge cornice sending hundreds of tons of snow two hundred metres over a crag into the coire below. Being so far away from the edge offered no chance of seeing any way through so with some trepidation I moved just a little bit further out toward the edge. A crack behind my feet appeared at much the same time as the sound. The noise of a big cornice breaking is like a gun going off, the noise went reverberating around the coire. Andrew and Dick were approaching the bothie and stopped and wondered; where might Richard be. I was air born, strangely calm and with time to think and consider that this was the end. It sounds trite but I felt regret for Barbara and the kids but being unable to influence events no real fear, that is until I started to become crushed and realised that instead of hitting something very hard I might finish up with an undamaged body buried and still conscious under tons of snow. I finished up being spat to one side of the avalanche debris as it expanded and ran into the coire bottom. With only an arm and a leg buried I struggled free. At the bothie Andrew asked if I had heard a cornice break, 'Yes, I replied, I just came down on it.'

It was an unfitting end to a really good winter, which had included a brilliant first ascent on Liathach, a mountain in Torridan where me and Andrew had climbed a 600 ft ice fall in perfect conditions on a glorious day, we called it Poachers Fall.

# 36

## A SPRING DAY IN GLENCOE

When I first moved north I was told that it was crucial to grab any good weather while it lasted, otherwise a year might pass without getting much done. The years since have taught me the truth of this statement. If you cannot skip a day off work, or climbing partners are in short supply then watching good weather pass is frustrating. In spring time there is often a good period of weather that can be warm dry and midge free. 1977 had been a good winter, in fact the weather for most of the year was good, but in that glorious spring there was no knowing what was in store. We had opened Barbara's pottery and before getting a job I could grab some time. George Sheilds stayed in Aviemore, maybe I could get him out. George was old school and vastly underrated. In George's youth, long before the climbing press existed, there were some very good climbers whom climbing history has passed over. As it happened he was doing repairs to his house so after helping for the afternoon I went off to Glencoe on my own. Even Rannoch Moor felt as if it might have dried out, the Coe smelt dry and warm. The weather the next morning was no different. A route called Carnivore had been on my wish list for ages, 600 ft E3 6a / 5c I was dragging a rope and a few slings and managed to back rope the first part of the traverse. At first the rock above was green but thankfully turned out to be dry, the climbing was open, not hard but without much respite and with poor friction it felt insecure. Above lay a band of overhangs, the Whillans finish climbed through these by an inviting dry crack. Believing this to be harder than the original finish, I continued by a traverse rightwards. A wide streak of wet mossy rock oozing out from under the overlap stopped progress. Mentally I had given up on the direct way but climbing across this wet streak was just not, for me, possible. Then I saw three old pitons in the wet crack, they had most likely been there since the first ascent in 1958 and were just rusty relics but they might hold a static pull. By joining some slings together to make two cow's tails I could remain clipped into the first peg while pulling on the second, having clipped this I then unclipped from the first piton reached across to clip the third. Taking as much weight on my feet as I could but a slip with either foot would have put a shock load on the pitons. After this gripping section the rest of the way up to a grass ledge is 5c, but my memory of this is blank. Stopping on the grass ledge was a mistake, the last pitch although only 4c was open and very airy and festering on the ledge had made me aware of where I was.

It was still only mid day, high up to the left of Great Gully, Slime Wall was displaying all 500 ft of her bone dry light grey rhyolite which is so often dark and wet. Although having had enough grip for one day I could not let this opportunity pass. I fancied a climb called Apparition, 500 ft E1 5b. The first part of Slime wall is always in the shade, I was wearing shorts and a T shirt so I started the climb shivering. After one hundred foot of easy climbing I was at the foot of the crux section of the climb, around 150 ft of 5a / b. The actual crux is a thin groove climbed on small good holds but on each move the next holds are not easy to see from below, never strenuous but with no handholds good enough to ever feel safe whilst I looked around. Above this pitch the climbing became easier as I emerged into the sun. Solo climbing so near the limit of your standard is hard to justify but the buzz is fantastic. It is not about having a death wish, on the contrary one's senses and awareness are acute and produce a feeling of euphoria and relief when you are safe again.

I now had two baby boys as well as Barbara to consider. It was a magnificent and beautiful day, a perfect swan song for solo climbing.

# 37

## THE ASSOCIATION OF BRITISH MOUNTAIN GUIDES

From somewhere I rustled up enough money for the train fare to Chamonix. I arrived in Argentière early on a Sunday morning with no tent or anyone to climb with. Geoff Arkless his wife Breda and Terry Taylor were all running courses for alpine novices, these courses were good and inexpensive. Geoff offered me work in exchange for food and a doss. I shared a tent with a guy called Mick Tighe who was working all summer for Geoff. Mick had just left the Marines and although we had never met he asked me why I was not in the Swiss Alps with his mates from 45 Commando. The previous winter two marines had caught us up on the Orion face of Ben Nevis. On the summit one of them had invited me to join them for twelve weeks in Switzerland. This would have been at Queenies expense. The man making me the offer was Dave Nichol, second in command of the Artic warfare cadre of 45 commando. The offer was too good to be true and I never took it seriously, so foolishly I never got in touch. Working with Mick, we did the Forbes arête on the Aiguille du Chardonnet and the ordinary route on the Argentière. It was a new experience using the Refuges for both eating, as well as sleeping. Being paid for climbing, good quality easy mountain routes devoid of any profound fear really appealed. I had briefly helped Breda back in '63 when she was running MA courses but they offered no continuity of work. Geoff, Breda and Terry had stayed the course ploughing their own furrow but this required a special kind of stoicism, which

I for one lacked. In the autumn I was climbing with a Welsh mate Phil Thomas, we found out that the Association of British Mountain Guides had decided to apply for membership of the Union International Alpine Guide Montagne. The name alone attracted us so we decided to apply for membership. I was working as a maintenance joiner in a hospital and the thought of running around the Alps doing what I wanted was too much to resist. I only knew about four basic knots but at least that was a start. My knowledge of navigation was zero. For now my climbing experience especially in the Alps was more important; the experience of the new aspirants could be used to good effect by the guides in their application to the UIAGM. The big stumbling block would be my medical background. Our GP on the Black Isle had known the famous climber / character Dr Tom Patey years before and this had got us on good speaking terms. Asking him to consider any kind of medical approval would put him in an onerous position; but I asked anyway. His positive response was life changing. He wrote to Iain Jones at Bangor hospital for a second opinion. Mr Jones was the surgeon who had saved my life fourteen years before. He replied in the positive, which said to use the formula that then pertained to the driving licence i.e. three years fit free. By now I had gone five years. The association accepted this and I began the series of three tests, summer, winter and alpine. The summer test came first. There were three of us, me Pete Long and my friend Pete Minks. Minks had just got back from the Himalaya with a badly sprained ankle, he should have waited for his ankle to get better and use the time to do some simple navigation. I had climbed the Freney pillar on Mont Blanc with Minks in '72 but amongst his exploits since was a solo ascent of the Walker Spur on the Grande Jorasses and only the year before he had climbed the North America wall on El Capitan. Before the test I needed to learn some navigation, but not having a clue I had to start at the most basic level. Bill Bowker had been working for years as chief instructor at an outdoor education centre in Wales catering for children. This was perfect for the job. Crawling through hedges and finding telephone boxes was good fun, a shame Minks was not with me. On the summer test we did the night navigation together, I passed and he failed. Considering Pete's very impressive mountaineering record, him failing the test was a travesty, but that's my opinion. Knot tying and improvised rescue I made a half reasonable job of but the navigation became harder for the winter test. The alpine test was enjoyable, assisting John Brailsford in the Ecrin. John ran an outdoor education course for would be instructors based in Bangor, he also did some private guiding. His contacts within the French Guides were very much the catalyst for the UIAGM looking favourably at the BMG's application for membership. When I was fifteen or sixteen the very idea that someday I would become a fully qualified alpine guide would have seemed completely improbable so I was immensely chuffed. In the Alpine areas, guides command a great deal of prestige, their job needs it. Money alone cannot recompense them for what is a very difficult and dangerous job. I had spent some time on the dole while I was doing the guides test and in the meantime we were skint so I got a job. I spent the next three years working as a labourer / rigger at the nearby, BBC transmitting station. Making a living as an alpine guide would have to wait.

Some mountain days in Scotland can be alpine in scale. The day Charles and Diana married the BBC gave everyone a day off work. Me and Clive Rowlands had spent the night before in the CIC hut with the intention of climbing all the ridges of Ben Nevis in the day. Starting up Raeburn's arête, a two hundred metre severe and continuing up North East Buttress makes a good climb of 500 m. By the time we finished crowds were gathering on the summit to celebrate the royal wedding, this continued throughout the day with more and more people appearing. We dispensed with the rope and climbed

MARMOLADA DI ROCCA SOUTH FACE, DOLOMITES 1984—THE GOGNA ROUTE FOLLOWS
THE PRONOUNCED ARÊTE IN ITS UPPER HALF—PHOTOGRAPH BY: AUTHOR

Observatory buttress a 340 metre V Diff. The descents between each climb were tricky in places, with hard patches of snow left from the previous winter. After Observatory ridge we climbed Tower ridge a 600 m diff. We then had a brew in the hut before finishing the day by Castle ridge a 275 metre mod. This gave a total for the day of 1,715 m of climbing. That same summer we did the traverse of the Cuillin ridge for the first time. Although not hard, as a mountain experience they are truly great and only a couple of hours drive from home

The flip side of guiding is that unless you are young and keen it is paradoxically not so good for your own climbing whereas even a short holiday away from an ordinary job can be productive. My holiday allowance on the BBC was limited to no more than two weeks at any one time but a month in total. This gave me the opportunity to have family time away and an alpine visit. Chamonix had changed, different campsites different bars made it difficult to meet old faces. New buildings had almost obliterated any farmland and hid the old town. John Vincent was not interested in bars or reminiscing about the sixties so we had a productive time. For the Swiss route on Les Courtes we stayed the night in the Argentière Hut. It was so different than sleeping out looking at your proposed climb scaring yourselves silly. Instead you leave the hut, stumble across the Glacier and in a sleepy haze, with hot coffee and bread inside you and before you are fully awake you are committed. Only later in the day with the crux behind us, the sun fully switched on and the snow mush, crampons skating on hard ice did we wish we were fitter and more acclimatised. Nonetheless as we crawled into a sleeping Couvercle hut with aching toes we were pleased. A far more amenable trip was the Cordier Pillar on the Aiguille Charmoz. Leaving big boots on a ledge we changed into rock shoes at the bottom of the climb. So different from the past, the climb was equipped for an abseil descent all the way from the top. The rappel points also made belays. The climbing was really good in particular

TUT BRAITHWAITE CLIMBING GOGNA ROUTE

PHOTOGRAPH BY: AUTHOR

TUT BRAITHWAITE BELAYED LOST IN THE MIST—GOGNA ROUTE

PHOTOGRAPH BY: AUTHOR

the top pitches. John was not keen to fester so we filled up the rest of the holiday with smaller things. The next year I went to the Dolomites with Tut. The weather on the whole was rainy but we did a good route in the Brenta Dolomites, put up by Bruno Dettassis before the war. The climb had some bold wall climbing which at the time of the first ascent gave it a difficult reputation. Bruno was still going strong running the refuge, not talking to German climbers because of his experiences fighting with the anti-fascist Italian partisans in the war. From the Brenta we went to the Marmolda and climbed the superb Gogna route on the south face. Four pitches from the top we were hit by a fierce hail storm. Two Italian lads, one a guide, joined onto our rope and with Tut doing a magnificent job of leading fought our way to the top where the sun came back out. The job with the BBC was very cushy but union demarcation nonsense got in the way of the foreman rigger using me as much as either of us wanted. Much of the time I was used as a forty odd year old brew boy so with bad timing I left in the autumn months before any winter work instructing. However over time this proved a mistake made in heaven.

# 38

## GOLD DUST

A rock fall from a crag onto the road had killed a highland regional councillor. Someone in the Dingwall office must have observed workers on alpine passes, abseiling down cliffs cleaning and netting the faces to prevent falling rocks and decided that this was the answer to the problem. Willy Sutherland from Carbost on Skye was the man. Within weeks Willy had notices up in job centres all over the central belt asking for anyone who might have done any abseiling or maybe even some rock climbing. This answered my lack of guiding work in the autumn of '83. This rock scaling job at Dornie must have been the first rope access job in Scotland. Willy supplied a harness, one rope per person and a figure of eight descender, no prussic slings or shunts. Locking off the figure of eight required a little jump upward whilst trying to push the rope over the top to lock it off, a difficult manoeuvre for beginners or on overhanging rock. With no safety back up rope, a severe cut to the working line could have been fatal. A lot of the youths who appeared were on the dole. Their experience was probably confined to a day abseiling in the scouts. They did not last long, Willy had no sentiment. Steinbeck would have had a field day, a *Grapes of Wrath* moment occurred every Friday afternoon when the lads who were not suitable stood trying to hitch a lift back home their belongings in a plastic bag. Some real climbers appeared, dragged from their life of indolence by the promise of good money, cash in hand with little chance of the dole finding out. Willy had some machines on the job, diggers and a JCB. Only one of the machines had an engine. I was pleased with the money and it was good fun. Willy's fiefdom was on Skye. Back in 1957 he had been the Youth Hostel warden when we spent our holidays there. Willy also had a self taught explosive expert that he could call on when he needed. His chance would come later but for now we happily abseiled about the rock face removing any loose rocks, the bigger the better. Marcus Barnes was the one who played the clown, always shouting with exuberance as with a crow bar in hand he caressed the rock. One time a sudden silence rent the air, Marcus had shut up. He had cut more than half way through his rope and with care he descended to the floor shaken. Another day he stuffed some overalls full of dead bracken and flung them off the crag in front of a car which was waiting by the traffic lights that we had in place. With the red bracken pushing out from hands feet and neck it looked like a decapitated body with blood spurting out. The weather was dry, the humour might be infantile but the craic was good and there were a lot worse ways of earning money. A rock in the shape of a flying buttress hovered over the road, perfectly sound but its removal would impress the council man on his weekly visit. Willy decided to have it removed by his explosives expert, his name for ever a secret. Dave Cummins, Jim Kerr and I worked as a team. Dave and Jim also became Guides and once qualified have lived in Chamonix for years. The top of the rock was a flat ledge, the three of us were instructed to drill big deep holes and put sticks of gelignite in them. We then had to link them together with some white cord. Willy's expert must have worked on the Hoover Dam because the amount of explosive he had us set was enormous. Before the detonation I ran half a mile down the road, the rest of the lads stood about twenty yards away. Most of the rock which blew into the air sailed straight over their heads and landed behind them, almost unbelievably none of them were injured. Soon afterwards I left; the winter climbing season had arrived and I had work guiding and instructing. Within a couple of

BARBARA AND OUR BOYS—SUMMIT OF GREAT GABLE

PHOTOGRAPH BY: AUTHOR

years rope access had really taken off. Twenty five years later some of the lads who stayed the course on the Dornie job are still working in rope access. For many climbers and cavers, especially those with limited employment potential, the gravy train had arrived.

# 39

## GUIDING

For an ambitious mountaineer, guiding can help to fund their lifestyle and keep a good level of fitness for their own ambitions. I was forty three when I started earning a living guiding full time, life had moved on and I had no big ambitions of my own. Since the early seventies climbing standards had risen to a level way beyond which I could ever have reached but I enjoyed instructing. There is a perverse pleasure in sleeping in a snow hole on the Cairngorm plateau, watching the moon come up towards Aberdeen or night navigating in a white out and finally finding the way back to a snow hole and a hot brew. It is good to pass on techniques and enthusiasm to beginners, or even experienced crag rats who want to get into winter climbing. Instructing an appreciative group of people can be so good it seems obscene to be paid. The down side is going out in any weather often doing the same climbs day in day out. Guiding individual clients where a good relationship has developed would be the ideal thing, but it could take years to collect sufficient number of clients with this proviso to make ends meet. There is a quote by Colin Kirkus, 'You know, Alf, going to the right place, at the right time, with the right people is all that really matters. What one does is purely incidental.' This quote by Kirkus is true whether with a friend or a client and to ignore it risks undermining the love you have for the hills. Most of my winter and summer work consisted of working on courses from either different centres or the BMC. This entailed running around the hills often with four people. To ensure that people

SON ALAN OFF PISTE SKI DESCENT ARGENTINA, 2009

had good value and were always secure, long winter routes would often finish after dark. My biggest weakness as a guide was that I was too frightened of the potential consequences of trusting relative beginners on easy ground, either unroped or moving together and I would often sacrifice speed for security.

After the guides had run the first few tests which they thought would satisfy the UIAGM Syllabus the Swiss observed that we had not included skiing. The aspirants, who got through the test before this anomaly was discovered and had the full guide's carnet, were exempted from the ski test. However it was felt that at least we should attempt to learn. For me the cost would be a problem, the equipment being out of our pocket. Then we discovered that every autumn there was a sale of second hand ski gear in Aviemore. At the time, lift passes on Cairngorm were not very expensive so kitted out from the Aviemore sale all the family started to ski. Our boys soon made better progress than me and Barbara and for several years we had some amazing days zipping and falling about Cairngorm. At the time there was a large rambling wooden cafe which would be full of damp people, tobacco smoke and hot chocolate. It was an atmospheric place with old timers like Plum Worrall with his hook nose and curly pipe. Unfortunately the building burned down a few years later. I can never drink hot chocolate without remembering those happy days. If I had not started on the path to becoming a guide, it is doubtful that we would as a family have gone skiing; it appeared to be too expensive but in Scotland lots of working people ski. I never progressed to becoming a good skier but I have always enjoyed the effortless way you can move about a mountain exchanging perspectives of the scenery in the twinkling of an eye. The boys both became competent skiers. Later as a grown man Alan became almost fanatical about skiing. Ian gave up both climbing and skiing and became a dedicated surfer. Ski Mountain touring in the Alps is even better, half the time is spent sliding uphill with skins

GUIDING ELLIOT'S DOWNFALL AONACH DUBTH, GLENCOE

GUIDING HAUTE ROUTE SWITZERLAND LATE 1980S

PHOTOGRAPH BY: JACK VAN DER SCHOOT

GUIDING HAUTE ROUTE SWITZERLAND LATE 1980S

PHOTOGRAPH BY: JACK VAN DER SCHOOT

on your skis, being able to stop and look at the view anytime you want, except of course in a white out. An offer came from my mate Bill Bowker wanting to know if I would like to do the High level route with him and two others. The journey is traditionally made from Chamonix to Zermatt with an option of extending the tour finishing in Sass Fee. Bill had decided on going the other way, starting in Sass and finishing in Chamonix. The trip was momentous and apart from a small late afternoon storm on the second day the weather was perfect. Every day of the journey is etched in my memory, as enjoyable as anything I have ever done. Nine days spent among the glaciers and peaks in windless completely clear blue skies. All the mountain refuges except one were manned and the food provided was always good. In the years since then that has nearly always been my experience. As young men it was a shame that we did not use the money that we spent on beer staying in the refuges. The Alps are different to other big mountain ranges of the world. Grazing cattle in the pre-Alps ensures the ground is covered in verdant grass with massive well built wooden chalets and barns. Trees are allowed to grow large for their timber. The extensive system of mountain huts is unique, disliked by purists but loved by people who enjoy comfort. There are hundreds of them, often in the most unlikely and remote positions. The majority sell good cooked food. In old age we have used them many times. Alpine huts hold many happy memories. A huge bonus for the years I spent guiding was the alpine hill walking we enjoyed as a family in between guiding commitments. On one occasion we did a multi-day trip called the Roma way in the Bregaglia range with two clients and a six-foot-six aspirant guide called Chris Dale helping. The highlight of which was meeting the legendary Walter Bonnati in the Ponti hut.

# 40

## ENVERS DES AIGUILLES

The place was crowded so we left our sacks outside the hut ready to pick up and go, the following morning. Most of the other people were friendly, everybody in the hut seemed to be crag rats going to climb the many bolted routes in the near vicinity so leaving our sacks unattended did not seem any risk. With my eldest son Ian we left the hut to climb a route called Le Marchand de Sable, reputed to be very good. Ian produced about four extenders out of his sack, I had none. It was like a kick in the balls, surely my trust in other climbers was not misplaced. Boots and crampons back on, we could have by-passed the hut on our way back to the valley but we thought we may as well have a brew. 'Why are you back?' Among the French, Elizabeth the hut warden had become an institution. I could hardly say that some thieving sod had nicked a pile of my gear so I muttered something about being forgetful. Without any fuss she insisted I borrowed ten of her extenders. Back at the start of Le Marchand as we were getting geared up again I found my own extenders hidden in a pocket of my sack. A year later myself and Ian went back to climb another route that she had recommended. For a present we took her a bottle of perfume, not very useful in the hills but she seemed flattered and pleased. Outside in the sun, a straw hat on his head sat an old French guy. The way Elizabeth danced attendance on him made it certain the man deserved respect. Lost for words about the perfume she instead introduced us to Lucien Beradini the charismatic guy in the straw hat. I was asked had we ever met before, without any thought of diplomacy I blurted out 'Yes, in a fight in the Scotch club in 1963.' Beradini had been on the first ascent of the west face of the Petit Dru in 1952, at the time a tour de force of western alpine aid climbing, and had lost toes and fingers after an epic on the south face of Aconcagua in the Andes. Instead of being annoyed he used my comment to inform everybody as to whom he was. 'I am the famous Lucien Beradini, who has done all sorts of stuff including losing half my feet and all the English man can remember me for is a fight twenty six years before.' At breakfast we shared the same table and seemed to be served twice as much coffee and bread as normal. He was still climbing, albeit with a Guide. At first our respective climbs lay in the same direction, without much comment he put his hand on my shoulder and pointed out mine and Ian's proposed climb as we came to it. Any bad feeling from all those years ago had been forgotten.

# 41

## INSIDE A CREVASSE

From the Bertol hut we headed for the Col du Valpelline. An Austrian Guide heading for the Dent Blanche stopped to talk. The snow conditions were good and our rope was an ornament as we walked along side by side talking and enjoying the morning whilst it was still cold. Paranoid that the Austrian was thinking that this was how the British Guides treated glacier travel I got us walking in line. In front was a family I knew, walking in line abreast, behind us a French couple, side by side. Unknown to any of us a storm a few days before had dumped a lot of fresh snow and the wind had created a nice cover over the biggest of the crevasses. A shout from the col warning us was only heard by me. Barry who was a bit deaf walked on. As he disappeared Colin was pulled off his feet and followed him. In theory my reactions were good, I fell on the snow and slammed the pick of my ice axe in the hard snow, at first it worked then slowly I was pulled forward, the pick of my axe slowly cutting a deep groove. Both Barry and Colin were suspended in mid air. The bottom of the crevasse was a long way underneath and was shaped like a barrel, the walls converging at the top and bottom. On entry I shot in like a rocket and slammed into the opposite wall head first. It was the only time that I had ever worn a crash helmet on a glacier. Barry and Colin were floundering about in soft snow at the bottom of the crevasse as I landed crampon first between them. Under this new snow the crevasse continued as a narrow slot into the bowels of the glacier. Once we had pulled ourselves into a safe standing position Barry asked quietly how we were going to get out. Even with the best of ice tools there was no way I could climb the seventy feet of overhanging ice, there were even lumps of fresh snow glued in places to the otherwise smooth walls. 'No problem Barry,' I had to bullshit big time to prevent panic seizing us all, and then a foot appeared overhead. The French girl had stopped for a pee and was rushing to catch her boyfriend up. If Barry had not been such a fat little bugger we might never have been pulled in and like the French girl, whose foot briefly appeared, would never have been aware of this enormous hole. Then like a mirage hundreds of feet away, sunlight penetrated the dark and the size of the walls appeared to diminish. We had to take care on the long traverse, front pointing and never stepping backwards onto the snow, aware that it was merely a soft bridge to eternity. The left wall turned out to be a fifteen foot slab and within a couple of hours we were having a brew with Dave Walsh, Sue and their boys in the Bouqetins bivi hut.

# 42

## ROPE ACCESS OFFSHORE

EMI is a small firm specialising in None Destructing testing of welds, NDT for short. They worked mostly on North Sea Oil and Gas platforms and wanted some of their men training in rope access techniques. In the four years since I worked on the rock scaling job at Dornie rope access had become much safer and methods were beginning to be standardized. This method of reaching the work site would over the next years go on to save millions of pounds by doing away with the need for always using scaffolding. Glenmore lodge trained some of their technicians and EMI now needed suitably qualified people to oversee safety and setting up the rope work. Guiding and instructing was patchy and time off was unpaid, if this offshore scam materialised it would be like finding El Dorado. I heard on the grapevine that interviews were being arranged for safety supervisors at Glenmore lodge but that Sunday was the last day to apply. That weekend I was working on a Winter Skills course in the northern coires of Cairngorm and it seemed impossible to get any spare time. Then the transit van of students I was with became stuck in a traffic jam. It started near Coylumbridge and finished at the car park at the Cairngorm ski area. Taking a chance I ran up to Glenmore, arranged an interview for the following week and ran back. The interview was in a warm hotel, Roger Donovan, chief instructor at Glenmore Lodge was in one seat, the boss of EMI, Danny Constantines was in another and in the corner seat sat a young women, legs crossed, short skirt, nice rounded knees, drawing on a fag in a fancy cigarette holder. Dawn Robertson did the hiring and firing. Her knees impressed me, but my mate Dave went working for another company CAN (offshore) in Aberdeen. My only experience of jummaring was on El Capitan 15 years before. A few days later we were in a sports centre in Fraserburgh, Roger emptied the contents of a bag of caving gear onto the floor with no explanation of how it worked. This stuff is definitely different from climbing gear, not surprising considering the troglodytes who invented it. We were going offshore the next day. After farting about for an hour I had some idea how it worked but hardly enough to be an expert. Sammy Crimble was a permanent member of staff at Glenmore lodge and was sent offshore with me and two techs, basically to see if what they had instructed was appropriate. The oil company was not too chuffed with this idea. Me and Sam were really non-producers and as such they only needed one of us. The problem, for them, was which one of us to get rid of. After arriving on the platform we had to wait in our cabin for an induction. Before this happened a man arrived and asked who was in charge. Rashly Sammy put his hand up and was then taken on a tour of the platform. Having toured this metal monstrosity until his head hurt the boss man asked Sammy if he could remember where the Radio room was. He was like most people put in this situation, clueless. Sam had become redundant. This was very lucky for me, Sam had a permanent job but for me this was a life changing opportunity. A year later I became probably the only man in North Sea history to fail a leg entry test. This test consisted of going down one of the Legs on Brent Delta and filling in a test paper on what was down there. I had wandered about, conscious only of being hundreds of feet beneath the sea and the sound of water dripping it was a totally alien world, seeing anything useful just passed me by. That first trip offshore on Viking 'A' gave us more money than we had ever had. At 47 years old spare money had appeared. The only blip on the horizon was the medical we all had to pass. I had

WORKING BY ROPE ACCESS METHODS DRILLING RIG CROMARTY FIRTH

PHOTOGRAPH BY: LES ABRAHAMS

CALLE
OLVIDO

no need to have worried; they must have been instructed to pass anyone who could walk through the door. In the next five years none of the doctors noticed that neither of my arms had more than about 30% of their potential range of movement. Although I had been free of epileptic seizures for 14 years I was still on medication, being frugal with the truth was one thing, getting my drugs offshore was another. Barbara solved it by sewing them into my clothes. A few years later we were waiting for a chopper in Sumburgh airport on our way out to the northern sector. A man in late middle age was fumbling with some change trying with no success to use a public phone so I offered help. The man had been bumped at the check in, the girl on duty claimed she could smell beer on his breath and refused permission for him to continue his journey off shore. This spelt disaster for him, at his age finding another job offshore would be difficult. He was trembling with shock but if he was still drunk he did not smell of booze as the girl had claimed. His words came tumbling out. He was scared shitless about arriving home and facing his wife, the gravy train gone; just another hard up couple in Glasgow. I got a line through to his employer in Aberdeen and handed him the phone. Then the tannoy beckoned us away. The pathos that man represented had shaken me and made me aware of the cushy bubble I had lived in since leaving the building trade. It also made me more paranoid about the drugs sewn into my clothes. We lived in our own house in the country side, bought before houses went expensive, Barbara was teaching in a secondary school and I was lucky enough to have the resources to be able to reinvent myself. The man who I had met in Sumburgh airport very likely did not.

# 43

## BOLTED CRAGGING

'Where do you get that stuff from?' I had gone for hand set radios to the radio room before working over the side. These radios were to communicate with the stand by boat in case we fell in the sea. The boat was about a mile or so away and could scarcely see us but rules are rules. It was a funny question to be asked by a portly radio operator sat in his warm base but apparently he had a house in Spain which needed the outside painting. Seizing the opportunity I offered the services of me and a mate Roy Warner. The man agreed, flight and food, and with the proviso that we could stay on and do some rock climbing for a further week. The house was in a mountain village with tiny streets and the whole place was built on a steep hill. The gable of his house backed onto a street set at thirty degrees or more to the horizontal. The difficulty and boredom of the job was improved by watching the locals going about their daily routine. One of the men, a builder, was fascinated by our rope manoeuvres and even helped by lending us a long scaffold tube. Benidorm was only a half an hour drive away and the whole area had become a mecca for bolt protected climbing. This massive departure from traditional ethics caused a lot of controversy but was the only way to protect the acres of pristine pocketed rock in places like the Verdon gorge or blank fantastic granite in the Alps. For me and Roy this purely bolt protected climbing on small crags was our first time and we were instantly smitten. Generally safe, usually sunny and with only a small amount of gear needed, it is both easier and less

CLIMBING MOTORHEAD, EL DORADO SWITZERLAND 1990

CLIMBING SEPTUMANIA, EL DORADO SWITZERLAND WITH SON IAN 1989

PHOTOGRAPH BY: DENNIS BURNS

effort than hiking up to a windy cold crag with heavy sacks. This is not a sentiment I would have had as a young man, for some perverse reason. The following summer, with our son Ian and Dennis Burns we went for a quick visit to the Grimsel Pass in central Switzerland to climb on the aptly named El Dorado. From the Grimsel Hospice it is a two hour walk by the side of a dark green dam. Unlike the river in Conrad's book *Heart of Darkness,* the dam led us not into jungle but equally menacingly toward a cirque of shadowy glaciated Oberland peaks, seemingly the most unlikely place to find almost two thousand feet of the most immaculate clean granite, south facing with an easy descent. That first visit, the three of us climbed Septumania. I went back to El Dorado a year later with our Ian and climbed Motorhead. A few years later I returned again with a friend Ian Fenton and climbed Forces Mortrice. Over the ensuing years Barbara and I have returned to climb at the nearby Handegg. That whole area of Grimpsel, Susten, Salbit and Furka is a granite wonderland. It must be said that many of these fantastic climbs would have very few runners or belays without bolts. In the Mont Blanc range dozens of these bolted routes have been equipped that never go near a summit but go up to some arbitrary spot and abseil down. A lot of these granite climbs are no bigger than Creag an Dubh-Loch or the Shelter Stone in Scotland. Although the Alps are a long way to travel not to be bothered scaling a peak but the scenery is fantastic and the sun is often out. Unlike traditional alpine routes where heavy sacks have to be carried up the climb, surplus equipment is left at the bottom to be retrieved after the abseil descent lands the climber where they began. The climbing is often strenuous, technical and generally with sustained difficulty. This is unlike many traditional alpine climbs that often have technically easy sections. With global warming shrinking the glaciers and easier mixed climbs, Alpine guides are now bolting more amenable easier climbs for their clients. The differences between the old challenges of only piton protected, shadowy Dolomite walls like the 3000 ft Civetta north face and these are immense, but to really enjoy a sunny day on the bolts it is worth while having spent time on climbs like the Phillip Flam.

# 44

## CROSS ROADS

Guiding and working on the oil rigs, was, at least for me incompatible. There was on the one hand the work in a sterile environment, stuck on a metal structure surrounded by grey sea and men who were often just marking time from one fortnight to another; two weeks on and two off and by comparison working as guide in a world of grand mountain scenery. Either one or the other entails being away from home for long periods of time but unless I could extend the guiding season, the money without also working offshore work was too insecure. Then Bill O'Connor offered me work in the Himalaya guiding trekking peaks. There were two seasons for this work, pre-monsoon and post-monsoon which did not interfere with either summer alpine or Scottish winter work and so would fill the year. Epilepsy had curtailed my only other trip to the Himalaya nineteen years before but was the enterprise worth the risk. Being completely new to the game I was dependant on the Sirdar for almost all the decisions. In retrospect I think he was concerned more with getting the job done quickly and getting paid than actually getting people to the top of our planned mountain. My lack of experience gave him a free hand. Our planned objective was a trekking peak called Pharchamo 6,187 m. The most straight forward route to the mountain is from the East but our route went by way of the Rolwaling valley to the west. One member of the team developed a very bad cough at the last village and to make up for lost time our Sirdar had us go from a low camp to the Tashi

Lapcha pass at 5,755 m in one massive push. I arrived totally knackered, the tents were already up but the porters dressed in any old gear were preparing to bivouac on some rocky ledges. In the night it started snowing, for me it was heaven sent, I felt shivery despite being in every stitch of clothing and a very good sleeping bag, I also had absolutely no energy. With the porters in rags and no tents, there was no way we could stop and wait for the weather to improve without risking their lives so we descended easily to the east. My altitude sickness did not improve as we lost height. As it transpired I would have very little energy for over a year despite spending a week in hospital in Inverness with nothing being diagnosed. At Lucla we had to push and shove for two days before we got a plane back to Kathmandu, and in the process I lost my medication. Getting out of the plane, the heat was oppressive and beggars were everywhere but the team insisted in going out for a meal. Sitting in a cafe was the last place I wanted to be; then I passed out. When I woke up a young German doctor who had been sat at the next table was speaking to me. I was unutterably disappointed. It had been years since I had last had a fit. After so long I had assumed they were gone forever. The decision to either stay guiding or work offshore had been taken for me, neither option was now possible, it all seemed a disaster. Then out of the blue there came an opportunity.

# 45

## IRATA

I could never have believed that this Himalayan disaster would have a golden lining, I was fifty two and without an obvious way of earning a living. Then the boss of a diving firm John Mackenzie appeared and wanted four of his divers training to pass the IRATA test for rope access. Weeks later the council sent four of their men to be trained. This was an opportunity sent from heaven. In the period that I had worked offshore the techniques and equipment were not very different from what they are now but the training was not to any standardized formula. Some of the firms in Aberdeen joined together and created an organization which they called the Industrial Rope Access Trade Association. There were, as now, three levels of expertise with the third grade being responsible for setting the ropes in place and any rescue. A climbing friend, Sandy Allen persuaded me to join him on a visit to Dent where the interviews and test were being held to create a body of assessors. This was caving territory in the heart of Yorkshire; how would two climbers from north of the border go down. The training committee, troglodyte cavers to a man turned out to be amenable enough and me and Sandy became approved assessors. For me this was an incredible piece of luck. For what seems so dangerous, rope access has a spectacular safety record, most of which is due to the training and assessment initiated by IRATA. I applied and became a registered IRATA training company. A local farmer had a huge shed used for storing grain, he allowed me to make a very good training area in it. The place was an old aircraft hanger and its large stanchions and huge angle iron roof trusses made, in my opinion, a top of the range facility. I made two large timber towers and bought an old portacabin and with nine hundred pound in my pocket went back down to Dent and bought the required gear from Lyon Equipment. For some weird reason they would only take cash. For ten years we ran a profitable good quality business. The job was especially satisfying because it got people into comparatively well paid work. By drinking gallons of tea and coffee and talking non-stop I effortlessly found a technique for getting men from entirely different backgrounds to get on with each other. The courses had five full days training and an assessment on the sixth day. We produced the first manual specifically for rope access training and the company earned a good reputation, most of the custom came by word of mouth. Some of the rescue techniques were developed by riggers on these early course such as Charlie Kennedy from Nottingham and Maurice Macleod from out west. Many trainees were from the Outer Isles, they were generally mild mannered but possess extra sensory powers which enable them to find their way without recourse to either timetables or watches. They are usually thoroughly good guys. I was now at home more than any time in the last ten years and Barbara, now in her fifties, started to rock climb again. The business was flexible enough for us to take advantage of her school holidays and sufficiently profitable for us to visit exotic climbing locations. It was like being young again. For the next twelve years several different types of anticonvulsant drugs never gave me absolute cover, meaning the length of a climb or general hardship of any scheme always had to be factored into the equation. The line between comfort and excess is often close and I had to choose comfort, not so bad really. The Pillar of Wisdom is a 300 metre climb on Jebel Rum in Jordan, for most of its length it is only grade 4 and 5 but the climbing is open and feels more serious than the grade. It would have been difficult to retreat from. The last few moves of the last pitch

BARBARA DESCENDING FROM THE BISHORN SWITZERLAND

PHOTOGRAPH BY: AUTHOR

PHOTOGRAPH BY: AUTHOR

BARBARA HANDEGG SWITZERLAND LATE 1990S

had a move of 6b protected by a manky bolt. Our belay at the start of the last pitch, was a large friend, when Barbara found the friend was stuck she scratched away at the soft rock until she could remove it. The top of Jebel Rum is like a sandstone glacier with the odd crevasse about a thousand foot deep. We had previously traversed the peak with our Bedouin guide, 'One Shot.' Tony Howard had given us a letter of introduction to a local guide called Abdul, what we did not know was that every male in the place was called Abdul and the one we met was the wrong one. He was however a happy chancer. After pocketing Tony Howard's letter he drove us off into the desert to meet his mum, en route a solitary bird appeared high in the sky. Abdul screamed to a halt rummaged under his seat for a single barrelled shot gun and brought the bird down with one shot. The inside of the tent was dark I was scared of doing anything that might be inadvertently bad mannered and sat slowly down on some blankets, which contained a baby. A few days later One Shot drove us to the far side of Jebel Rum in his jeep and showed us the way up Sheikh Hamdan's route to the summit of Jebel Rum and down Sheikh Hammad's route back to Rum village. On the summit we found some five gallon plastic water containers. He insisted that his mother would be so chuffed with these we could all carry one on the descent. On the first abseil he insisted on climbing down, solo, with two of these containers. On that pitch he needed rescuing but lower down the descent he reversed some long pitches faster than we four abseiled them, muttering something about him being fine providing he stayed on the right side of Allah. On mine and Barbara's descent from the Pillar of Wisdom dehydration was playing funny tricks with my mind and before long we were lost. This was despite detailed instructions from a French climber as to how to join the Hammad descent. I knew there were cairns leading to our descent but I insisted in scurrying about at the bottom of the sandy Wadis. Then we found a small stagnant pool. After a drink my mind cleared and we found the descent complete with abseil points and got down about midnight.

Any grand ideas of alpine classics had to be tempered by my responsibilities so we preferred mid grade climbs of moderate length in places like Tuolumne meadows in California, Spain, Switzerland, Italy and France. On a visit to the Orny hut in the late 90s we climbed a nine pitch route with some moves of 6b on the Petit Clocher du Portalet, last year, 2009 we went back to the Orny hut and climbed a ten pitch 5+ on the Aiguille Orny. In the years between we have had countless good days. After several different types of drugs my doctor found one that worked. My right hip had become arthritic and both hill walking and jummaring up ropes was becoming harder. Regretfully I sold the business. Two years later I got a new hip; it is a brilliant success. Just recently I was looking through the vast guide book library of a fellow member of the British Mountain Guides who lives in Chamonix, I remarked on how much climbing there is out there to do and by comparison how little I had done. His reply was a mild rebuke as he observed that even after two lifetimes there would still be plenty of places to go and routes to climb. In a way he was suggesting that in old age I should reflect on virtually thousands of marvellous days out in the hills that I have had and how a climber could go on and on without ever being satisfied. Mark Charlton's comment rang a bell, from crawling along on my hands and knees on the Cuillin ridge as a sixteen year old to doing many big climbs. Adrian Burgess reminiscing about alpine climbing in the sixties remarked that it was often like being in a war zone. It was not said in any macho self regarding way but a bald statement of the truth, reflecting on the gear available the paucity of information and the training routine of being drunk whenever possible. My years working as a Guide and instructor were often very enjoyable and satisfying, running the rope access training business made me feel useful and the last twenty years climbing with my wife an unexpected bonus.

Most climbing books describe monumentally difficult achievements or major epics. I hope I have described the life of an ordinary crag rat and of all the other climbers I have met along the way. For fifty five years the sport has brought me joy that many people can only dream of and the company of a thousand and one individuals. I feel immensely lucky and chuffed to have been a part of it.

*'Far off and faint as echoes of a dream the songs of boyhood seem.'*

*'And when he can no longer do more than lift his eyes to the hills he will still find that the promised strength is unfailing — not of body, but of spirit, garnered from long days spent in natures tranquillity and peace.'*
Taken from the book by Andre Roch, 'On Rock and Ice'.

# ACKNOWLEDGMENTS

•••

Having beavered away for ten years and having finished up with a book bigger than the bible, I was persuaded to cut it down to its present size. In doing so I have lost many events and omitted some good friends to whom I apologise.

But beware this is merely volume one.

•With Special Thanks to

Barbara McHardy
Ian and Alan McHardy
Rory Maclean
Dia Mouratidou
Sandy McGregor
Will Fraser
Sandy Allen
Sinclair Fraser
The Late Ed Grindley
Brian Barlow
John Brailsford
Steve Dean
Malcolm Creasey
Leslie Boulton – For talking me into buying a laptop and Christelle Panquet for teaching me how to use it

•Also With Thanks For Providing Pictures to

Bev Stevens
Andrew Dowset
Ackers Atkinson
Andy Garvey
Leo Dickenson
Chris Bonnington
Gordon Stainforth
Les Brown
Peter Cliff
Paul Ross
George Homer
Dennis Burns

Les Abrahams
Jack Van Der Schoot
Dave Tidmarsh
Reg Phillips

# INDEX

•••

# INDEX

•••

# INDEX

•••

CLIMBING THE CORKSCREW PINNACLE UTAH 2002

PHOTOGRAPH BY: PAUL ROSS